Curriculum
Integration

DESIGNING THE CORE
of
DEMOCRATIC EDUCATION

Curriculum Integration

DESIGNING THE CORE
of
DEMOCRATIC EDUCATION

James A. Beane

Teachers College, Columbia University
New York and London

Published by Teachers College Press, 1234 Amsterdam Avenue, New York, NY 10027

An earlier version of Chapter 3 appeared as "Curriculum Integration and the Disciplines of Knowledge," in the *Phi Delta Kappan*, 76(8), 616–622. Reprinted with permission.

Library of Congress Cataloging-in-Publication Data
Beane, James A., 1944–
    Curriculum integration : designing the core of democratic
education / James A. Beane.
        p.   cm.
    Includes bibliographical references (p.) and index.
    ISBN 0-8077-3684-8 (cloth). — ISBN 0-8077-3683-X (pbk.)
    1. Curriculum planning—United States.   2. Curriculum change—
United States.   3. Critical thinking—Study and teaching—United
States.   4. Interdisciplinary approach in education—United States.
I. Title.
LB2806.15.B43   1997
375'.001—dc21   97-26139

ISBN 0-8077-3683-X (paper)
ISBN 0-8077-3684-8 (cloth)

Printed on acid-free paper
Manufactured in the United States of America

04   03   8   7   6   5

Contents

Acknowledgments

In the two years spent writing this book, I often tried to think about how I have come to believe so firmly and confidently in what it is about. It would be dishonest to say that it was entirely a matter of empirical investigation or deep philosophical rumination. A fair share has been more like intuition, but not blind intuition, because the fact of the matter is that I have spent my life in the presence of progressive educators. My mother, Kay Beane, was a progressive teacher in the 1920s and 1930s, and she and my father, John Beane, carried that philosophy into their childrearing practices and their work on many projects in the school district I attended. I literally heard this stuff at the dinner table as I grew up. My mother also kept many of the records from my schooldays that now remind me of some of the teachers I had: Karle Wicker, who planned with his fourth-grade students; Fran Waggoner and Dorothy Volgenau, who used a project approach complete with self-evaluation procedures as part of the junior high school core program; and Ed Larson, who taught his high school students about social inequities and injustice. I think it is time that I acknowledged their work and the fact that I did not learn about progressive teaching only after I left school.

Along those same lines, I have now come to more fully appreciate what I learned from colleagues early in my professional career. Robert Lux, my teaching partner, literally showed me how to use the disciplines of knowledge in an issue-centered curriculum, while our team conversations with Sue Jarosz, John Slattery, and others taught me almost everything about the debates surrounding progressive teaching. Meanwhile, my professors at the State University of New York at Buffalo, Conrad Toepfer and Bob Harnack, taught me about the theories involved in curriculum integration and "core" curriculum, as did my fellow graduate student and friend, Sam Alessi (who still knows more about all this than I do). I think it is about time that I acknowledged that I did not learn about progressive education and curriculum integration only after I left full-time teaching and graduate school.

During the years that I have been a professor, I have learned more and more about this kind of work from colleagues: Phil Eberl, Peggy Burke, and

Dick Lipka at St. Bonaventure University; Janet Miller, Ed Mikel, Gail Burnaford, Smokey Daniels, Ethel Migra, Marilyn Bizar, Linda Tafel, and others at National–Louis University; and, through professional associations, Ken Bergstrom, Elizabeth Pate, Michael James, Sue Thompson, Ed Brazee, Richard Powell, Nancy Doda, Jim Ladwig, Jan Phlegar, Nancy Spradling, Larry Craig, Nancy Nagle, Glenellen Pace, Tom Dickinson, Camille Barr, John Arnold, Chris Stevenson, and many more. With regard to many of the ideas in this book, I am especially indebted to two people. One is Gordon Vars, longtime "keeper" of the progressive core curriculum, who offered numerous suggestions for this book. The other is Michael Apple, who has patiently tried to teach me about the politics of curriculum organization and the uses of knowledge. I think it is about time that I acknowledged that these people are not so much colleagues as they are my teachers.

Over the past several years, I have spent considerable time with teachers who use the idea of curriculum integration, including the feature of planning the curriculum with students: Mary Ploeser, Gary Weilbacher, Cathy Gilmore-Nelson, Lori Neubauer, Carol Smith, Alice McVetty Vars, Amy McClellan, David Debbink, Elaine Homestead, Kathy McAvoy, Dennis Carr, Carla Jacobs, Lynn Moss, Pat Sinkiawic, Lorraine Schoepfer, Donna Spurlin, and many more. Some were kind enough to review chapters of this book, especially Chapter 4, in which I try to capture what I have seen in their classrooms and what they have told me about their work. A few even let me teach with them. They probably have no idea how much it means to me that they treat me as a colleague. But most of all, in this regard, I am indebted to Barbara Brodhagen, whose theoretical grasp and pedagogical skill with this work is pushing us all forward. The fact that I happen to be married to her means that I get the benefit of living in the midst of a constant tutorial. I want to be absolutely clear in acknowledging that among the countless lucky students these teachers have had, I am one.

In my judgment, no theory of education can be considered complete or even adequate without taking into account the stories of young people. Lately I have learned a lot by listening to Dan, Lisa, and Jeff Liebergen; Tim, Ali, Jamie, and Brian Brodhagen; Tedd and Annie Herman; Holly and Dan Meyer; and David Vierling. I have been treated with great kindness by so many young people in the schools here in Madison, Wisconsin, and elsewhere around the country. I wish I could name all of them. But most of all, I have understood both my theories and my commitments in light of what I learned from the school experiences of Jim and John Beane, and Jason Vigneri-Beane. There would be no sense in trying to hide this even if I wanted to. Anyone who reads this book will know immediately that I could not possibly have learned all that is in it from adults alone.

Introduction

I first became interested in the idea of curriculum integration in 1967 when my major professor, Conrad Toepfer, suggested I read two books by L. Thomas Hopkins, *Integration: Its Meaning and Application* and *Interaction: The Democratic Process*, as well as works associated with the "core curriculum" movement. These were "old" works, left over from progressive education efforts in the 1930s, 1940s, and 1950s. But as a young teacher I was drawn to them and so tried out ideas, such as the problem-centered approach, the project method, and teacher–student planning, that were featured in discussions about curriculum integration, democratic schools, and the "core" approach. In the 1970s and 1980s, however, these views of curriculum design were pretty much marginalized in public and professional discussions about education and in the field of curriculum studies itself. True, there was work beyond the separate subject curricula going on in early childhood classrooms, in the whole-language movement, and in "interdisciplinary" projects in some middle schools, high schools, and universities. But it was certainly not in the mainstream of educational currents.

This is hardly surprising, since curriculum "reform" had taken a quite different direction in the midst of larger conservative movements. Competency-based education, "back to the basics," management by objectives, increased graduation requirements, and schemes for more classical courses were all the rage (and still are, to some extent). Meanwhile, the field of curriculum studies had moved boldly into the arena of cultural politics, a move whose timing was all the more important as the conservative restoration advanced. But the matter of straightforward curriculum design and organization was often relegated to courses on the history of curriculum as scholars spent their time debating the political motives of earlier design theorists.

Imagine my surprise in the late 1980s, then, when the term *curriculum integration* suddenly popped up in professional literature and on conference programs. How could it be that this approach, with its glaringly progressive roots, could emerge in a time that was so decidedly conservative and when the attention of progressive curriculum theorists was turned in another direction? As it turns out, there was little to be surprised about. While the idea of curriculum integration had emerged earlier in the century in relation to such ideas as social integration, democratic class-rooms, wholistic learning theory, and the integration of knowledge, its late-twentieth-century version was reduced to the matter of correlating content and skill from various subject areas around some theme. This was certainly a safe definition—apparently safe enough even for the conservative restoration—and many of the kinds of curriculum units and projects that were springing up around it were exciting and engaging. Moreover, most progressive curriculum theorists did not seem to object.

However, this was not what I had understood "curriculum integration" was meant to be. And such a limited (and incorrect) definition of the approach cut off conversations before getting to really progressive possibilities. It was one more example of how progressive ideas get redefined so that they fit painlessly into more conservative traditions in school and society. I must confess that I was very angry over this. It all seemed so unfair. Those earlier progressives had fought hard to make a place for ideas such as curriculum integration, and some had paid a serious professional price for their views during the right-wing attacks in earlier times. How could this important history be so easily erased?

I finally decided to write this book for three related reasons. First, while the small book I wrote in 1990, *A Middle School Curriculum: From Rhetoric to Reality*, was based on the theory of curriculum integration, I did not deal explicitly with the theory itself and its place in general education at all levels. Second, given the current misinterpretation about curriculum integration, the time seemed right to put forth a "biography" of the concept to try to set the record straight about what it was meant to be. And third, I wanted to expand and extend the theory of curriculum integration using some of the ideas that I had learned working with the design inside and outside of classrooms for over 30 years.

Given the present confusion about the meaning of curriculum integration, it is possible that someone might come to this book expecting to learn about the overlaps or connections among school subjects and how to create thematic units out of them. This would not be surprising, since the term *curriculum integration* has too often been used to describe arrangements that amount to little more than rearranging existing lesson plans. This is unfortunate because, since its beginnings in the 1920s, curriculum integration was intended to mean much more than that. Curriculum integration is a curriculum design that is concerned with enhancing the possibilities for personal and social integration through the organization of curriculum around significant problems and issues, collaboratively identified by educators and young people, without regard for subject-area boundaries.

In curriculum integration, organizing themes are drawn from life as it is being lived and experienced. By using such themes, the way is opened for young people to inquire critically into real issues and to pursue social action where they see the need. That inquiry and action add depth to the meaning of democracy in schools, which curriculum integration further emphasizes through its emphasis on collaborative teacher–student curriculum planning. Such collaboration also opens the way to redefining power relations in the classroom *and* to challenging the idea that important knowledge is only that named and endorsed by academicians and bureaucrats outside the classroom.

Curriculum integration also involves applying knowledge to questions and concerns that have personal and social significance. In doing this, the boundaries between separate subject areas are dissolved and knowledge is repositioned in the context of those questions and concerns. Scope and sequence of knowledge are thus determined by the questions and concerns collaboratively planned by teachers and students. Since knowledge is pushed to the level of problem solving and other forms of application, young people are frequently engaged in "performing knowledge," an experience that may range from presentations to social action. Because knowledge is actually put to use, young people are pressed toward higher standards as they confront more challenging skills and forms of content. This repositioning of knowledge also requires flexible use of resources drawn from both popular and high culture.

Finally, with its emphasis on participatory planning, contextual knowledge, real-life issues, and unified organization, curriculum integration provides broad access to knowledge for diverse young people and thus opens the way for more success for more of them. For those same reasons, it offers a curriculum that most young people see as worth their time, effort, and attention. It is little wonder that so many teachers, parents, and young people have come to see this approach as offering the more challenging content, the higher standard, the world-class education that is so often talked about but so rarely experienced.

Someone who has never worked in a school or been in on some kind of curriculum reform might ask what could be wrong with that description or how anyone could object to it. But those who have worked in schools know very well that no alternative to the traditional high-culture, subject-centered approach, no matter how good it sounds, has a comfortable place in the curriculum. There are always critics both inside and outside the school. And even when the classroom door is closed, no kind of teaching, especially progressive forms, is easy to do. So it is that despite many successes over more than 70 years, work around the idea of curriculum integration continues to be contentious. Nevertheless, more and more teachers are expressing interest in the idea, and numerous accounts of its use in classrooms around the country are appearing in books and journals.

In the first three chapters of this book, I concentrate on the "idea" of curriculum integration. Chapter 1 lays down the theory of curriculum integration. This includes an explanation of the four major themes of the theory—the integration of experience, social integration, the integration of knowledge, and integration as a curriculum design. It also includes discussion of how this approach differs from others that are beyond the traditional subject curriculum as well as an explanation of the sources of organizing centers or themes for curriculum integration.

Chapter 2 explores the history of curriculum integration. I am aware that some people find such history lessons tedious, but it is here that we find the grounds for moving with confidence beyond the ahistorical and distorted definitions of curriculum integration that have gained currency in current professional circles. In Chapter 3, I take on one of the most contentious debates around curriculum integration, namely, the fate of the disciplines of knowledge as subject-area lines dissolve. Here I hope (though not unrealistically) to put to rest the prevailing but incorrect observation that knowledge from the disciplines disappears in curriculum integration. In fact, I argue that the disciplines of knowledge are likely to find more legitimacy than they have now in the curriculum and in the judgments of young people.

The next two chapters focus on the matter of what it is like to do curriculum integration. The first of these, Chapter 4, grows out of my experiences in classrooms working alongside or observing teachers using this approach as well as what they have told me and/or written about their work. Specifically, I explore what seem to be the topics that teachers most often talk about as they use this approach with students: collaborative planning, performing knowledge, organizing and using knowledge, creating communities, and relationships. I also suggest what I sense are the kinds of beliefs that these teachers carry with them into their classrooms: beliefs about young people, about learning, about knowledge, about the purposes of education, and so on. Then, in Chapter 5, I take up some of the contentious aspects of curriculum integration, beginning inside the classroom and school and extending out to academic, bureaucratic, and cultural politics.

In Chapter 6, I turn back to the larger question out of which the idea of curriculum integration originally emerged: What should be the general education offered in schools in a democratic society? Here I argue that the curriculum of such a general education would be organized around major social issues, would engage young people in using knowledge to work critically on those issues, and would involve large doses of localized collaborative planning by teachers and their students. In that way I hope to explain once more what curriculum integration was meant to be about while also pointing to the philosophical and pedagogical corruption in most current work on a so-called "national" curriculum.

Finally, in the last chapter, I discuss the two major dilemmas curriculum integration faces as its advocates call for wider use of the approach. One is its lack of bureaucraticizing structures in an era when powerful interest groups seek centralized authority over teaching and learning. The other is the ways in which its fundamental values contradict those of dominant, privileged groups in the society. At the same time, however, I want to argue that curriculum integration fares well today because of the commitments of its advocates. On a scholarly note, I have tried to assemble here a bibliography on curriculum integration that is as historically complete as possible. Thus those in search of "leads" on related work should notice bibliographic sources that are pertinent to curriculum integration but not cited in the text.

Finally, and again, for those who think that curriculum integration was meant to be about rearranging content from several subjects around some theme, this book may come as a shock as they discover that the idea involves much, much more. As I have said elsewhere, curriculum integration is not simply about doing things differently, but about doing something really different. I hope that those people are not scared away by this but rather are encouraged to press further in their work. As for those who come to the book knowing more fully about curriculum integration, especially teachers who use the approach, I hope they feel that I have spoken well and accurately for their work. That I hope for especially.

CHAPTER 1

A Special Kind of Unity

Suppose that we are going to work with a group of students on a unit about "Environmental Issues," including major concepts or "big ideas" such as conservation, pollution, politics, and economics. What kinds of experiences might best help young people address these issues? To explore the concept of conservation, students might work on school or community recycling programs, make recommendations for resource conservation after studying waste patterns in the school or community, and/or carry out a multimedia campaign to encourage conservation and recycling in the school and community. To explore the concept of politics and the environment, they could carry out a survey in the school and community regarding attitudes toward issues such as recycling or land use, prepare exhibits that display competing viewpoints about environmental issues, and/or research how debates about environmental issues have changed over time. To explore the concept of pollution, they might test water or soil from nearby sources, survey businesses and industries about efforts to reduce pollution, and/or prepare exhibits on various kinds of pollution.

Having completed our work on that unit, suppose we next organize a unit on "Living in the Future," with related concepts such as technology, living spaces, health, and others. Here students could conduct a survey on beliefs held by peers about the future, tabulate the results, compare them to other forecasts, and prepare research reports. Or they might look at technological, recreational, entertainment, or social trends and develop forecasts or scenarios for the future of one or more of those areas. Or they could research past forecasts made for our own times to see if they actually occurred. Or they might develop recommendations for the future of their local communities in areas such as population, health, recreation, transportation, conservation, and so on. Or they could study the effects of aging on facial features to imagine how they might look when they are older.

Now, it does not take much more than a cursory reading of those examples to see how the young people involved in them would be engaged with an enormous range of knowledge, from information to values, and including content and skills from several disciplines of knowledge. Yet in the process of describing activities to address various concepts, I did not categorize them by various subject areas. Instead, knowledge was integrated in the context of the "environment" and "future" themes and the activities within them. In those contexts, moreover, knowledge took on an immediate importance and purpose. In this case, the answer to the usual student questions about why certain skills or concepts have to be learned is not "to prepare for some future" but to do what needs to be done *now*.

This classroom scenario has several distinguishing features. Its organizing centers are significant problems or issues that connect the school curriculum with the larger world. The organizing centers serve as a context for unifying knowledge. Knowledge, in turn, is developed as it is instrumentally applied to exploring the organizing centers. So organized, the curriculum and the knowledge it engages are more accessible and meaningful for young people and thus more likely to help them expand their understanding of themselves and their world. Of course, all curriculum designs claim to create connections of some kind or another—with the past, with the community, across subjects, and so on. But here is a curriculum design that seeks connections in all directions, and because of that special kind of unity, it is given the name *curriculum integration*.

Philosophers and educators have always been concerned with "integration" inasmuch as that term connotes the tension involved in part–whole relationships. In the 1800s the idea of integration in relation to schools was focused on the school's role in promoting social unity, or "social integration," especially as the idea of common, public schools gained ascendance. In the late 1800s, followers of the German educator Johann Herbart developed ideas about correlation of subjects that were sometimes referred to as "integration of studies." By the mid-1920s, however, "integration" had assumed a new meaning as organismic, and Gestalt psychologists had introduced the concept of an integrated personality and described processes by which people supposedly sought unity among their behaviors and values, between self and environment, and so on. It was this meaning of "integration," explored in a 1927 dissertation by Meredith Smith, that helped shape a crucial question: *Are certain curriculum organizations or approaches more likely than others to assist young people with the processes of personal and social integration?* Responses to that question took three directions.

One response suggested that the process of integration would be facilitated by a child-centered curriculum that drew its direction and organization from the child's interests, experiences, and "development." One example of this was the "activity curriculum" in which children were encouraged to draw their own conclusions from activities that involved observation, hands-on experimentation, and the like (Kilpatrick, 1934). Another was the "experience curriculum" in which teachers and students cooperatively planned activities around real-life situations with skills and concepts learned from carrying out the activities (Hopkins, 1941). Advocates claimed that these approaches aided integration by their focus on the students' own ways of organizing their ideas and experiences.

They also insisted that integration was something that people must do for themselves. For this reason they advised that the term not be used in relation to adult efforts to reorganize school subjects. Nevertheless, another response came from educators who were already interested in correlations across various subject areas and who often referred to those correlations as an "integrated curriculum." This response suggested that students were more likely to learn subject matter if it was organized into generalized concepts that cut across the fragmenting boundaries of separate subjects. So, for example, two subjects might be brought together in a "broad-fields approach" course such as humanities, skills might be reinforced across two subjects such as science and mathematics, or fragmented parts of a discipline might be "fused" to form a broad subject such as social studies (Hopkins, 1941).

Still another response to the question about integration and curriculum came from those progressives whose interests were focused on social issues and the concept of social integration. These educators supported the idea of personal integration and creative individuality but saw them as aspects of a democratic society rather than ends in themselves. Thus they questioned whether a completely child-centered curriculum would be truly integrative if it focused only on the individual process of integration and did not explicitly address the process of social integration. After all, the argument went, schools were supposed to be concerned with social improvement and the common good. Moreover, the "real life" with which the curriculum was supposed to correspond involves social as well as personal concerns (DeBoer, 1936). With a focus on social issues, advocates of this response framed what one called "the democratic integration process" by which the process of organizing experience and knowledge around social issues and situations might be done by groups as well as individuals (Cary, 1937). Thus the term *integration*, usually associated with psychology and knowledge organization, was also part of the movement for democratic education, including the popular problem-centered "core" curriculum (Rugg, 1936, 1939; Hopkins, 1941; Macdonald, 1971).

Given the treatment of curriculum integration in recent literature, speeches, and workshops, some people might find this brief historical sketch surprising. Current talk about curriculum integration is almost completely ahistorical, suggesting alternately that it is rooted in reforms of the 1960s or that it is a recent "fad" that began in the late 1980s. Furthermore, the same current talk almost always implies that curriculum integration is simply a matter of rearranging lesson plans as overlaps among subject areas are identified. Neither interpretation is true, of course, but the fact that both are widely believed has seriously limited discussions about curriculum integration and the scope of its use in schools.

DIMENSIONS OF CURRICULUM INTEGRATION

As it is meant to be, curriculum integration involves four major aspects: the integration of experiences, social integration, the integration of knowledge, and integration as a curriculum design. By looking inside each of these, it is possible to imagine how all are brought together—"integrated," as it were—in a comprehensive theory of curriculum integration that is more significant and promising than the curriculum arrangements that are incorrectly identified as "integration" in too many current discussions.

Integration of Experiences

The ideas that people have about themselves and their world—their perceptions, beliefs, values, and so on—are constructed out of their experiences. What we learn from reflecting on our experiences becomes a resource for dealing with problems, issues, and other situations, both personal and social, as they arise in the future. These experiences, and the schemes of meaning we construct out of them, do not simply sit in our minds as static, hardened categories. Instead they are fluid and dynamic meanings that may be organized one way for dealing with one issue, another way for a second issue, and so on. This kind of learning involves having constructive, reflective experiences that not only broaden and deepen our present understandings of ourselves and our world but that also are "learned" in such a way that they may be carried forward and put to use in new situations (Dressel, 1958). In short, what I will call *integrative learning* involves experiences that literally become part of us—unforgettable learning experiences. Such learning involves integration in two ways: first, as new experiences are "integrated" into our schemes of meaning and, second, as we organize or "integrate" past experience to help us in new problem situations.

The crucial issue with regard to this theory is, of course, how to organize curriculum experiences and the knowledge they engage in such a way that young people may most easily integrate them into their schemes of

meaning and carry them forward. Iran-Nejad, McKeachie,
(1990) suggest that too many educators believe that "simplifie
access to) knowledge is best achieved by presenting it in sma...
pieces. But a growing body of research suggests that access is mos.
through "integration" of details, that is, by organizing through "w.
ideas." They put it this way:

> The more meaningful, the more deeply or elaboratively processed, the more
> situated in context, and the more rooted in cultural, background, meta-
> cognitive, and personal knowledge an event is, the more readily it is under-
> stood, learned, and remembered. (p. 511)

In too many cases, the notion of learning that schools seem to promote is quite different from this. Instead of seeking meaningful integration of experience and knowledge, both are treated as a kind of "capital"
for accumulation and cultural ornamentation. Knowledge is dispensed with
the idea that it is to be stored away for future use, either to hand back in
the form of test answers or displayed when the occasion suggests. If this
seems too harsh, how else do we explain the responses young people get
when they say, "Why do we have to learn this?" "Because you will need
it for the test," their teachers reply. Or "for next year." Or, depending on
the moment, "for college or middle school, or high school, or work." Or
"You'll find out later in life." Dewey (1938), whose concept of experience
and education the theory of integration follows, put the matter this way:

> Almost everyone has had occasion to look back upon his school days and
> wonder what has become of the knowledge he was supposed to have amassed
> during his years of schooling . . . but it was so segregated when it was ac-
> quired and hence is so disconnected from the rest of experience that it is not
> available under the actual conditions of life. (p. 48)

Social Integration

Among the important purposes for schools in a democratic society is that
of providing common or shared educational experiences for young people
with diverse characteristics and backgrounds. The idea of such experiences
has long been tied to the concept of integration through emphasis on a
curriculum that promotes some sense of common values or a "common
good" (Smith, 1927; Childs & Dewey, 1933; Rugg, 1936; Hopkins, 1941;
Hanna, 1946; Beane, 1980). The portion of the school program devoted
to this purpose of "social integration" has often been referred to as "general education" because it is meant for all young people regardless of background or aspirations. It is this general education that is the site of debates

over what ought to be required of all students or what all young people should "know."

While most people seem to think general education should amount to a collection of required subjects, many educators and activists committed to social reform have called for other types of arrangements. Most prominent among these has been a curriculum organized around personal and social issues, collaboratively planned and carried out by teachers and students together, and committed to the integration of knowledge. These kinds of arrangements are promoted not simply because they make knowledge more accessible for young people but because they help to create democratic classroom settings as a context for social integration.

For example, the use of a problem-centered curriculum follows from the idea that the democratic way of life involves collaborative work on common social issues. The participation of young people in curriculum planning follows from the democratic concept of participatory, collaborative governance and decision making. The inclusion of personal issues alongside social problems follows from the democratic possibility of integrating self and social interest. And, as we will soon see, the integration of knowledge follows from the idea of the democratic use of knowledge as an instrument for intelligent problem solving (B. Smith, Stanley, & Shores, 1950).

No doubt some would argue that ideas like social integration are simply an anachronism among the late-twentieth-century identity movements that seem to defy the very concept of shared educational experiences. Setting aside the fact that progressive visions of general education recognized that individuals would take away different meanings from a common experience, that argument would imply that social integration and the related idea of democratic schools were once tried on a large scale but eventually became irrelevant. The sad fact is that both social integration and democratic practice have largely eluded the schools. Worse yet, the schools and their traditional curriculum organization have too often been among the persistent sources of inequity and "disintegration" found across the whole society.

However, it is possible to identify both past and present examples of democratic schools in action. Not surprisingly, these accounts almost always involve the concept of social integration (usually in the form of attempts at developing "classroom communities"), the integration of school and community life, and the use of problem-centered, integrative curriculum designs (e.g., Apple & Beane, 1995; Wood, 1992; Zapf, 1959). It is in this context of democratic social integration that we see the most powerful use of the concept of curriculum integration. Yet that context is rarely included in popular talk about curriculum integration today. This is not really surprising given the nearly complete lack of historical grounding in such talk or the fact that attempts at democratic social integration are more complicated than prepackaged "integrated units" and certainly more dangerous politically.

Integration of Knowledge

When used in relation to curriculum, *integration* also refers to a theory of the organization and uses of knowledge. Imagine for the moment that we are confronted with some problem or puzzling situation in our lives. How do we approach the situation? Do we stop and ask ourselves which part of the situation is language arts, or music, or mathematics, or history, or art? I don't think so. Instead we take on the problem or situation using whatever knowledge is appropriate or pertinent without regard for subject-area lines. And if the problem or situation is significant enough to us, we are willing and anxious to seek out needed knowledge that we do not already have. In this way, we come to understand and use knowledge not in terms of the differentiated compartments by which it is labeled in school, but rather as it is "integrated" in the context of the real problems and issues.

The isolation and fragmentation of knowledge is part of the deep structures of schooling. This is evident in the subject-specific curriculum documents, schedules, and other artifacts of middle and high schools and in the separate subject/skill schedule in so many elementary school classrooms. This latter point is important because it is too often assumed that the elementary school curriculum is not as subject-defined as that of the middle and high schools. Yet the structure of a self-contained elementary school classroom, like the structure of "interdisciplinary" teams in middle and high schools, too often hides a schedule in which the first hour is for language arts, the second for arithmetic, the third for another area, and so on.

When the integration of knowledge is advocated in schools, it is usually argued on grounds that it makes knowledge more accessible or more meaningful by bringing it out of separate subject compartments and placing it in contexts that will supposedly make more sense to young people. As we have already seen, a growing body of research evidence suggests that such "contextualizing" of knowledge does make it more accessible, especially when those contexts are linked to the life experiences of young people. Important as this is, however, it is not the only argument for the integration of knowledge in curriculum organization.

Knowledge is a dynamic instrument for individuals and groups to use in approaching issues in their lives. In that sense knowledge is a kind of power, since it helps give people some measure of control over their own lives. When knowledge is seen simply as a collection of bits and pieces of information and skill organized by separate subjects or disciplines of knowledge, its uses and its power are confined by their boundaries and thus diminished. For example, the definition of problems and the means of addressing them are limited to what is known and deemed problematic within a particular subject or discipline. When we understand knowledge as integrated, we are free to define problems as broadly as they are in real life and to use a wide range of knowledge to address them.

Moreover, as I will argue more fully later, one among many criticisms of the separate-subject approach is that it largely includes only the knowledge that reflects the interests of high-culture social and academic elites. Since the separate-subject division of knowledge focuses only on topics within the subjects themselves, other kinds of issues and knowledge are prevented from entering into the planned curriculum (Bernstein, 1975). On the other hand, when we organize the curriculum around self and social issues and draw upon knowledge that is relevant to those issues, knowledge that is part of everyday life as well as what is often called "popular culture" also enter the curriculum. The addition of everyday and popular knowledge not only brings new meanings to the curriculum but also fresh viewpoints, since it frequently reflects interests and understandings of a broader spectrum of the society than do the school subjects.

When what counts for worthwhile knowledge is confined to that annointed by scholars in academic disciplines and others of the dominant culture, organized in ways that are convenient to them, and presented as a kind of "capital" accumulated for some future time or for cultural ornamentation, two things happen. First, young people are led to believe that important knowledge is abstract from their lives. Second, they are deprived of the possibility of learning to organize and use knowledge in relation to issues that concern them. Educators thus become implicated in an education that is not only narrow and incomplete, but unethical.

Thinking in this way about the integration of knowledge and its uses as an instrument for addressing real problems is one sign of a deeper meaning behind the idea of curriculum integration, namely, its possibilities for helping to bring democracy to life in schools (Bellack & Kliebard, 1971; Apple & Beane, 1995). While the idea of democratic schools is usually taken only to mean the use of participatory decision making, its extended meaning includes attending to the issues, problems, and concerns that confront the larger democratic society. This aspect of the democratic way of life involves the right, obligation, and power of people to seek intelligent solutions to the problems that face them, individually and collectively. And for this purpose, the integration of knowledge is especially suited.

Integration as a Curriculum Design

The fourth way in which the term *integration* is used is to refer to a particular kind of curriculum design. As we saw earlier, the design named "curriculum integration" has several features that, when taken together, distinguish it from other approaches. First, the curriculum is organized around problems and issues that are of personal and social significance in the real world. Second, learning experiences in relation to the organizing center are planned so as to integrate pertinent knowledge in the context of the organizing centers. Third, knowledge is developed and used to address the organizing center currently under study rather than to prepare for some later test or grade level. Finally, emphasis is placed on substantive projects and other activities that involve real application of knowledge, thus increasing the possibility for young people to integrate curriculum experiences into their schemes of meaning *and* to experience the democratic process of problem solving.

To these features, I would now add one more that has long been associated with the concept of integration in the curriculum, namely, the participation of students in curriculum planning (e.g., Hopkins, 1941). If integrative learning is a serious intention, it is important to know how young people might frame the issues and concerns that are used to organize the curriculum as well as what experiences they believe might help them learn. It is hard to imagine how adults might find about how any particular group of young people view these matters without somehow consulting them directly. Just as importantly, since curriculum integration is tied to the larger concept of democratic education, the matter of student participation in planning their own experiences must eventually become a crucial aspect of the design.

This definition of curriculum integration as a curriculum design may surprise some educators who, in workshops and professional literature, have seen the term applied generically to any approach beyond the strict separate-subject curriculum. Unfortunately, such confusion over terminology has surrounded the concept of integration in the curriculum since the 1930s and, as we shall see next, continues today.

ELSEWHERE BEYOND THE SEPARATE SUBJECTS

In the present round of interest in curriculum integration, two issues not only confuse its meaning but also threaten to undermine its use in schools. The first is the misapplication of the term *integration* to what is actually a "multidisciplinary" curriculum. The second is confusion over the sources of organizing centers or themes that are used in curriculum integration.

Multidisciplinary and Other Approaches

Curriculum integration is obviously quite different from the separate-subject approach that has dominated schools for so long. It is also different from other arrangements and designs that are, to some extent, beyond the strict separate-subject approach and to which the term *curriculum integration* is often misapplied. For example, the term has been used in attempts at reassembling fragmented pieces of a discipline of knowledge, such as creating social studies out of history and geography or whole language out of fragmented language arts. It has also been used with regard to addressing things such as thinking, writing, and valuing across subject areas. One might argue semantically that the word *integration* is technically acceptable in these situations, but this is clearly not what has been meant historically by "curriculum integration."

Another way in which the term *integration* is used is in relation to "the integrated day," a method used in some British primary schools since the 1960s (Jacobs, 1989). In this case, children are given a say in the order of events during the schoolday and the amount of time devoted to each. However, as Paul Hirst (1974) pointed out:

> That pupils plan how long they devote to something and the sequence of things they will do is perfectly compatible with a highly subject structured curriculum. An integrated day may, or equally may not, involve an integrated curriculum. (p. 133)

Those uses aside, the greatest confusion has to do with a very different curriculum design that is often, and mistakenly, labeled as "curriculum integration" but would more accurately be called "multidisciplinary" or "multisubject." One way of illustrating the difference between these approaches is to contrast the ways in which they are planned. In curriculum integration, planning begins with a central theme and proceeds outward through identification of big ideas or concepts related to the theme and activities that might be used to explore them (see Figure 1.1). This planning is done without regard for subject-area lines since the overriding purpose is to explore the theme itself. In a multidisciplinary or multisubject approach, planning begins with recognition of the identities of various subjects as well as important content and skills that are to be mastered within them. A theme is then identified (often from within one or another subject) and approached through the question, "What can each subject contribute to the theme?" (see Figure 1.2). In this way, the identities of the separate subjects are retained in the selection of content to be used, and students still rotate from one subject to another as content and/or skills from each are correlated to the theme. Moreover, though the subjects are taught in relation to the theme, the overriding purpose is still the mastery of content and skills from the subjects involved. In this sense, the theme is really a secondary matter.

Figure 1.1 Schematic Web for Curriculum Integration

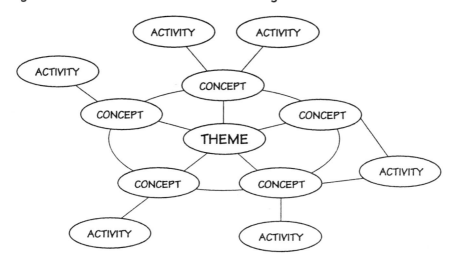

The fact is that the multidisciplinary approach to curriculum is really not very far removed from the separate-subject one. Again, even as planning around an organizing center proceeds, the identities of the separate subjects are retained (J. H. Young, 1991/1992). And as multidisciplinary units are carried out, students still experience a daily round of separate subjects in which the teachers more or less attempt to relate subject areas to the organizing center. This is very different from curriculum integration, in which students move from one activity or project to another, each one involving knowledge from multiple sources. But more than this, the two approaches, multidisciplinary and integration, are distinguished by deeper differences. Like the separate-subject approach, the multidisciplinary one still begins and ends with the subject-based content and skills while curriculum integration begins and ends with the problem- and issue-centered organizing centers (Bellack & Kliebard, 1971). Along the way, these organizing centers also contextualize knowledge and give it significant purpose. Because the multidisciplinary approach begins with content and skills, knowledge is fixed in predetermined sequences, while integration recognizes external knowledge but sequences it by relevance to the problem at hand.

Distinguishing between curriculum integration and multidisciplinary arrangements is not merely a semantic game; in fact, it is crucial for a very practical reason. Since curriculum designs beyond the separate-subject

Figure 1.2   Schematic Web for Multidisciplinary/Multisubject Approach

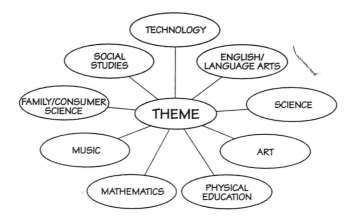

approach are so unfamiliar to most people, including most teachers, it is important that they understand the fullest range of alternatives. If multidisciplinary arrangements are mistakenly named as "curriculum integration," then the discussion of alternatives may stop before the possibility of real curriculum integration is made known. As discussions about curriculum organization develop and labels multiply, a pretty reliable way to figure which is which is to check for the root word *discipline*, which refers to the differentiated categories of knowledge that subjects represent. Where that root word is used—*multidisciplinary, interdisciplinary, cross-disciplinary*, and so on—something other than curriculum integration, usually a realignment of the existing subjects, is almost always intended.

I do not want to demean the multidisciplinary approach to curriculum here. In fact, its use has brought dramatic progress in many schools. As teachers have carried out multidisciplinary units, they have been more likely to use culminating activities that are project-centered and that call for the use of knowledge from all subject areas involved. In planning such units, teachers of different subjects frequently discover that they cover common skills and concepts. This often leads to simultaneous teaching of those skills and concepts in the subjects involved and the use of common assignments to show students connections between subjects. Since any such connections are likely to help students to some extent, multidisciplinary discussions across different subjects are very important. And in most middle and high schools where teachers in different subject departments often barely know each other, such discussions are nothing short of miraculous (Siskin & Little, 1995; National Association of Secondary School Principals, 1996).

It is worth noting that subject-loyal teachers frequently rebel more over contrived use of their areas in multidisciplinary arrangements than over the prospect of a real integration of knowledge. This is probably due to the fact that multidisciplinary arrangements retain the identities of subjects and, therefore, imply no changes in content coverage or sequence. In moving away from subject identities, the idea of really integrating knowledge reduces the need for contrived arrangements. As Dewey (1900/ 1915) advised:

> All studies grow out of relations in the one great common world. When the child lives in varied but concrete and active relationship to this common world, his studies are naturally unified. It will no longer be a problem to correlate studies. The teacher will not have to resort to all sorts of devices to weave a little arithmetic into the history lesson, and the like. Relate the school to life, and all studies are of necessity correlated. (p. 32)

Understanding these differences may also help us to clarify another issue in current discussions about alternatives to the separate-subject approach. I refer here to popular attempts to describe many alternatives, each with its own finely shaded description. This proliferation of "types," usually set along a continuum, has in some ways overly complicated the field. Beyond that deeply structured, separate-subject design, the crucial question is this: As we create new designs, will we or won't we attempt to retain the identity of the separate subjects? If yes, then the resulting design will be multidisciplinary. If no, if we are willing to let go of those distinctions, we may find our way to curriculum integration. While there may be many shades and variations within them, when it comes to the fate of subject matter, there really are but these two alternatives.

Organizing Centers

As interest in alternatives to the strict separate-subject approach has grown, it has become fashionable to claim that "Our school is using a thematic approach." While this may seem like a good thing on the face of it, such a claim raises the question of where the themes come from and how they are identified. The fact is that there are several sources of curriculum organizing centers beyond the separate subjects, and in the matter of integration, some are more promising than others.

One source of organizing centers is topics that are already contained within the separate subjects and covered in that approach to curriculum. Here, for example, are such topics as "Colonial Living," "Metrics," "Transportation," "Myths and Legends," or "The Middle Ages." The use of topics from within the existing curriculum, particularly historical periods, has been prominent at the elementary and middle school levels for years and is now of growing interest to high school educators. Obviously such organizing centers are popular largely because of their familiarity and the implication that the usual content will still be covered.

Another source is social problems or issues, such as "Conflict," "The Environment," "Living in the Future," or "Education." Social problems have been used as organizing centers by progressive educators for years, but others often shy away from them because such themes shift the focus from covering content to solving problems and because they may seem controversial in the conservative context of many schools.

A third source is the issues and concerns of young people themselves, including such issues as "Getting Along With Peers," "Life in School," "Choosing a Personal Future," or "Who Am I?" The concerns of young people are often used as organizing centers for set-aside arrangements of "affective education," such as advisory programs. This is at least partly because many educators simply cannot imagine that the agendas of young people themselves could or should have a place at the center of the curriculum.

A fourth source is what we might call "appealing topics," such as "Dinosaurs," "Apples," or "Teddy Bears." Topics like these have been popular at the elementary school level and to some extent in middle schools, and they usually involve projects and other interesting activities. However, the use of this source always raises two questions. One has to do with whether such topics have enough significance to warrant the amount of time devoted to them (Edelsky, Altmeyer, & Flores, 1991). The other question concerns to whom, exactly, the topics are supposed to be "appealing," the students or the teacher. One case to which this question might apply, for example, is the currently popular use of the 1960s as a theme, a decade in which many of today's teachers just happened to have spent their own adolescence.

A fifth source is process-oriented concepts, such as "Change," "Systems," or "Cycles." These concepts are different from the other sources in that they are about processes that apply to virtually everything rather than about a particular topic. This source of themes is somewhat puzzling since curriculum organizing centers are intended to provide students with concrete unity and coherence. Perhaps it is the fact that process concepts seem to apply to everything that makes them popular among those seeking a way to invite colleagues beyond the separate-subject approach. This may also be why they are most often used in relation to multidisciplinary arrangements. The problem with process-oriented concepts is that in applying to almost everything, they are not about anything in particular. For this reason they might be useful as strands within more concrete themes, but not as themes themselves.

Any of these types of organizing centers can be used with either a multidisciplinary approach or curriculum integration, *if we define the latter simply as a matter of disregarding subject-area lines in planning.* However, if we understand curriculum integration in terms of its larger meaning and implications, then the concerns of young people and social issues emerge as the sources most clearly tied to integration. After all, personal and social concerns are quite literally the "stuff" of life and likely to be the organizing schemes young people already use for knowledge and experience. Thus the familiarity and recurrence of such organizing centers may make "integration" all the more probable and meaningful. As Dressel (1958) suggested:

> Perhaps the extent to which a student perceives his own personal pattern of educational experiences as interrelated among themselves and as related to the problems and experiences presently and probably to be engaged in outside of school has more to do with the encouragement of integrative growth than any other single factor. (p. 21)

In the end, organizing centers that are not related to significant self and social issues may be interesting, fun, exciting, and even likely contexts for correlating separate-subject content, but they will not do if we really mean to engage in curriculum integration. William Smith (1935) put the whole matter this way:

> In order to be real, a learning situation must meet certain conditions: (1) It must revolve about problems which are germane to youth; (2) it must be concerned with vital and crucial aspects to the world in which youth is learning to live; and (3) it must call for dynamic and creative behavior on the part of the learner. A sound curriculum would thus consist of a succession of natural and vital units of experience, each centering about a real problem, each drawing upon subject-matter as needed, irrespective of boundary lines, and each eventuating in growth in capacity to live. The development of such a curriculum obviously calls for more than bringing subjects together into friendly relations under one teacher or, by way of so-called correlation, under several teachers. The essence of integration lies in the use of subject-matter by the learner rather than by teachers. It is a dynamic and creative process. (p. 270)

THE CURRENT INTEREST

The 1990s have been marked by a renewed interest in curriculum integration. Why this is so is a matter of some curiosity, especially since the general mood of this era is decidedly not in the direction of a progressive movement such as the one in which curriculum integration was initiated. However, a number of factors have converged to give the idea of integration some serious momentum.

First among these factors is growing support for curriculum arrangements that involve application of knowledge rather than merely memorization and accumulation. The move away from simple accumulation has support among a somewhat odd mix of advocates, including educators disenchanted with low-level learning and bored students, business leaders interested in applied knowledge skills such as problem solving, various groups calling for higher standards and more challenging content, and evaluation specialists concerned about authentic assessment.

A second factor is interest in new ideas about how the brain supposedly functions in learning. According to widely reported research, the brain processes information through patterns and connections with an emphasis on coherence rather than fragmentation (Macdonald, 1971; Caine & Caine, 1991; Sylwester, 1995). Those who advocate integration from this research claim that the more knowledge is unified, the more it is "brain-compatible" and, therefore, more accessible for learning. Interestingly, in the 1930s round of interest in integration, Hopkins (1941) and others warned that there could be no guarantee that any organization of knowledge by adults would necessarily be compatible with the integrative processes of young people. The new research suggests that this earlier admonition may have been somewhat overstated in that even correlation alone seems to make knowledge more accessible for students.

A third factor is the emerging sense that knowledge is neither fixed nor universal. I refer here to the postmodern and poststructural fascination with multiple meanings of language and action, and with the idea that knowledge is socially constructed. In the late twentieth century, it is getting increasingly hard to think of an answer to the question of what knowledge is of most worth when nothing is more certain than uncertainty, when yesterday's truth is repealed by today's discovery, which, in turn, is clearly in danger of tomorrow's breakthrough. As a curriculum approach that made its living off the claim of having all the answers (and the right questions), the separate-subject approach has never been on shakier epistemological grounds.

Related to this third factor is the recognition among a growing number of scholars that problems of real significance cannot be solved out of a single discipline of knowledge and, therefore, that it is increasingly necessary to look at the world across disciplines (Klein, 1990). For example, how is it that problems in the environment, in human relations, in medical ethics, and so on can be resolved by work within a single area? The answer is that they cannot. And what is the sense of having a curriculum that acts as though such problems are not on the minds of the young or that their consideration must begin with mastering a smattering of isolated facts from different subject areas rather than with the problems themselves.

A fourth factor is the continuing presence of those educators who maintain a serious interest in progressive educational ideas. This group would include, for example, advocates of "whole-learning" arrangements, such as whole language, unit teaching, thematic curriculum, and problem- and project-centered methods. It would also include those who recognize the social problem focus and the instrumental uses of knowledge in curriculum integration as an aspect of democratic education (Apple & Beane, 1995). And, too, it would include representatives of subject-area associations and projects, including in mathematics and science, who have called for ending fragmentation within their areas and connecting them to larger problems and issues.

In naming this collection of supportive factors, I am not claiming that all individuals or groups associated with any one of them support curriculum integration as I have described it. For example, the attitudes and skills that business leaders want schools to promote may fit well with the applied knowledge and project aspects of curriculum integration but not necessarily with ideas like the critical use of knowledge or the emphasis on economic equity within democratic social integration. Similarly, the concept of democratic social integration is likely to be entirely distasteful for those postmodernists who would argue that democracy is about difference rather than unity. As a collection, however, those supportive factors generally contribute to a climate in which it is possible for those who are interested in real curriculum integration to pursue their work. Moreover, the fact that there are multiple sources of support means that there may be many positions from which people will find their way to curriculum integration.

Ironically, many educators today like to speak of change in terms of "paradigm shifts" they have made or are trying to make. Such shifts most often seem to involve things like changing the school schedule, more sharply defining outcomes of schooling, or coming up with new methods of assessment. I understand the meaning of paradigm shift to entail a change in viewpoint so fundamental that much of what is currently taken for granted is now called into question or rendered irrelevant or wrong (Kuhn, 1962). So defined, it is hard to take the kinds of changes just mentioned as paradigm shifts. These, like most of the changes usually associated with "restructuring," ask only about "how" we do things and leave alone more fundamental questions about "what" we do and "why."

Curriculum integration centers the curriculum on life itself rather than on the mastery of fragmented information within the boundaries of subject areas. It works off a view of learning as the continuous integration of new knowledge and experience so as to deepen and broaden our understanding of ourselves and our world. Its focus is on life as it is lived now rather than on preparation for some later life or level of schooling. It serves the young people for whom the curriculum is intended rather than the specialized interests of adults. It concerns the active analysis and construction of meanings rather than merely assuming the validity of others' meanings. And it brings the idea of democracy to life through its problem-centered focus, its uses of knowledge, and its participatory framing. Described this way, curriculum integration involves something more like a real paradigm shift than what has usually passed for such.

CHAPTER 2

Looking for Curriculum Integration

Whenever educators gather to talk about curriculum integration, they ought to take a moment to remember that they stand on the shoulders of giants. Too many people seem to think that the idea is an invention of the late 1980s. They apparently don't know that the present work on curriculum integration follows that of many theorists whose published works since early in the century still have much to teach us. And, too, they are evidently unaware of the thousands of teachers and other educators, lesser known to fame, whose work on curriculum integration in local classrooms and schools has been a great pedagogical story in this century. It is hard not to feel angry when contemporary educators suggest that curriculum integration is "like what we did in the 1960s," or "what they did at Summerhill" (which they didn't), or, as I heard a presenter at a conference say, "interdisciplinary, integration, multidisciplinary—all those terms mean the same thing." I have tried to cite works from across the years not only because they are informative but also to remind us of the long tradition.

What is this tradition? Simply put, it is the search for an integrative curriculum—one that promotes the integration of experiences, of knowledge, of school and the larger world, of self and social interests, and so on. In this chapter I want to look at how curriculum integration has evolved over time. In doing so, I will stay close to my earlier definition of curriculum integration as a curriculum design theory that is concerned with enhancing the possibilities for personal and social integration through the organization of curriculum around significant problems and issues, collaboratively identified by educators and young people, without regard for subject-area lines. As always, this is not meant to completely reject other alternatives to the separate-subject approach, such as the multidisciplinary one, but to recognize that curriculum integration has a particular meaning and purpose that are not the same as those of other approaches.

It is important to note that this review is not a history of teaching techniques. While certain methods are implied by the curriculum integration concept, they are not the sole property of that design. For example, it is entirely possible to plan for activities and resources with students within a strict subject-area organization (even though some separate-subject loyalists would claim that young people cannot possibly have anything to say about subject matter they have not yet met). And presenting information or skills to students in relation to questions they have raised does not at all contradict the meaning of curriculum integration. No doubt certain methodologies are more apt to be used by teachers who lean toward curriculum integration, but it is the reasons behind their use rather than the methods themselves that are of interest here.

Also, I have chosen to limit this review of curriculum integration in two other ways. One is that it focuses largely on the United States. As will be noted later, there is a great deal of work available from many other countries, but I intended this review to have the special purpose of addressing the lack of historical perspective in the present movement for curriculum integration in the United States. Second, the review is limited to K–12 schools. This is not because there is no such history in higher education. Indeed, some of the most interesting cases of integration have occured in colleges and universities (Klein, 1990; Klein & Doty, 1994), and many currently support the same kind of work in schools through innovative ways to review the work of high school graduates who do not have traditional subject-based transcripts. However, the focus of this book is on K–12 schools, and to introduce the higher education picture would require at least another volume.

Ideas about curriculum do not evolve in a vacuum. Instead they occur in the context of larger movements within and beyond education. Beginning in the late 1800s, explosive expansion in industry, urbanization, transportation, and other areas gave rise to serious debates over the shape and future of public affairs, including the role of social institutions. In the area of schooling, those debates were compounded by the sharp rise in many school enrollments brought on by the mix of immigration, urban growth, child labor laws, and compulsory attendance regulations. The question of what kind of schooling was called for by these changes led to several reform efforts that would eventually frame the four major camps in what Kliebard (1986) describes as the twentieth-century "struggle for the American curriculum." Into the 1890s, the entrenched tradition in curriculum, basically the only game in town, was a combination of the high-culture subjects associated with classical humanism and the tenuous theory of mind-as-muscle psychology known as mental discipline. The overriding question raised by the reform movements was whether that tradition should continue or be replaced by curriculum forms that would serve "modern" purposes.

One such movement had to do with using the school to meet alleged "needs" of the emerging industrial society. In this case, following the lead of industrial efficiency experts, some educators recommended a differentiated curriculum to prepare youth for various roles in the adult world. So, for example, young males would be guided toward careers in either manual labor or management and the professions, while females would be offered a dose of domestic "science" along with the basic subjects. As with ability-tracking arrangements in our own time, it is not too hard to guess which combinations of race, class, gender, and/or immigration status led which young people to be "guided" into which tracks. Obviously this curriculum position was meant to serve not only labor needs but continuation of dominant class and cultural interests as well.

A second movement had to do with growing interest in children themselves, ranging from the romanticism of Rousseau to the "scientific" studies of children by G. Stanley Hall and others. The organization of the curriculum around adult interests, whether in the form of classical humanism or social efficiency, was deemed "unnatural" and thus in need of replacement by arrangements that more nearly matched the so-called "natural" developmental interests of children and adolescents. This argument would become a major battle cry of those who advocated for "child-centered" education, and it remains so today. However, two issues, largely unaddressed by this position, have always left it wide open for criticism and even ridicule. One is the accusation that in serving children's interests, the schools would ignore larger social purposes (as if adults would ever easily give up their interests for those of children anyway). The second issue is the puzzling use of the word *natural* to describe the interests of young people, as if they somehow develop apart from experiences in a world whose cultures and stratifications are anything but natural.

A third reform movement had to do with how the school might fit into the larger movement to expand democracy and assuage the social and economic inequities that were becoming more pronounced as industrialism expanded. With this idea, social reconstructionists gave a political edge to the milder concept of shared values involved in the "social integration" advocated by Herbert Spencer (1870) and others. Advocates of this position called not only for ending inequities in school structures but also for using social problems to help organize the curriculum, connecting the school with community issues, and more widely using democratic practices in school planning and governance. In these ways, the schools might not only stand as exemplars of democracy but also graduate young people who would be inclined to practice and work for the democratic way of life. That issues of race and class were sometimes given superficial treatment, and gender virtually ignored, suggests that the meaning of "democracy" in school reform was more than a little slippery, though perhaps not as elusive as it often seems today (Apple & Beane, 1995).

Despite the differences among these reform positions, each would eventually claim curriculum integration as a desirable way to organize educational experiences. For social efficiency advocates, the idea of integrating academic and vocational knowledge and applying it in real-life contexts was very attractive. For child-centered developmentalists, ideas such as personal integration, pupil–teacher planning, and project-centered learning were nearly enough to make an educational anthem. And for social reformers, social integration, collaborative planning, and the use of integrated knowledge to approach social problems offered a practical agenda for democratic education.

PUSHING PAST THE SUBJECT APPROACH

Amidst the swirl of reform, the separate-subject approach to the curriculum came under increasing attack. Before the turn of the century, members of the Herbartian Society called for the correlation of separate subjects around "cultural epochs" that matched the sequence of schooling with that of the development of "civilization" (DeGarmo, 1895; C. A. McMurry, 1895). So, for example, various subjects for young children could be correlated around early history, a period the child in "early" stages of human development could presumably relate to. Questionable as this developmental theory might be, it was attractive to many critics of the fragmented, decontextualized array of subject matter and skills in which students were drilled (Kliebard, 1986).

Another reform-minded educator, Colonel Francis Parker, demonstrated his interest in child- and problem-centered methods in schools in both Quincy, Massachusetts, and Chicago, Illinois. While loosely involved with the Herbartians, he was less interested in cultural epochs than in correlation and coherence in relation to the experiences of children themselves. Parker was already sounding the major themes of the later "integration" movement before the turn of the century. As suggested in a comment by a leading Herbartian (F. M. McMurry, 1927), Parker "was searching for the problem or project of work, where you find your starting point for both curriculum and method within the child rather than within some branch of knowledge" (p. 331).

And most powerfully, John Dewey argued for consideration of both the experiences of the child and social issues in organizing an educative curriculum, through writings such as *The School and Society* (1900/1915), *The Child and the Curriculum* (1902), *How We Think* (1910), *Interest and Effort in Education* (1913), and *Democracy and Education* (1916). Equally important were reports of the Laboratory School he directed at the University of Chicago, where, among other arrangements, the curriculum was organized around areas of human activity dubbed "occupations." To understand the place of Dewey in this line of work and the degree to which he anticipated misinterpretations, it is worth using once more the quote I cited in Chapter 1:

> All studies grow out of relations in the one great common world. When the child lives in varied but concrete and active relationship to this common world, his studies are naturally unified. It will no longer be a problem to correlate studies. The teacher will not have to resort to all sorts of devices to weave a little arithmetic into the history lesson, and the like. Relate the school to life, and all studies are of necessity correlated. (1900/1915, p. 32)

The term *integration* was rarely used in this early work on curriculum organization. In the 1912 *Cyclopedia of Education*, edited by Paul Monroe, an entry titled "Integration of Studies" referred the reader to an alternate heading, "Correlation," the term left over from the Herbartians. Meanwhile, social efficency theorists, who advocated for a linear and piecemeal curriculum, expressed hope that graduates would eventually unify and apply their fragmented school learnings through "final integration" (Dutton & Snedden, 1912). And "integration" continued to be used in relation to "social integration" (e.g., Inglis, 1918), as Dewey (1916) and others encouraged more active consideration of the schools' role in expanding the democratic way of life. However, near the close of the second decade of the century, major events unfolded that continued to lead in the direction of explicit attention to what I have described as "curriculum integration."

The fundamental debate among the four curriculum views described earlier had to do with what should constitute the general education program of the schools or the so-called "common learnings" that would involve all young people at any given level of schooling. Despite rumblings from the three reform positions, however, the classical humanism position that elevates a collection of subjects/disciplines to an end in itself still defined the substance of general education. In 1918, however, the National Education Association (NEA) Commission on the Reorganization of Secondary Education recommended a set of seven personal and social aims for the curriculum. Though these aims were to be accomplished largely through various subjects, classical humanism as a philosophy seemed at last taken down from its pedestal. For the upcoming idea of curriculum integration, this event would prove especially important. Then as now, arguing against a separate-subject curriculum would have been far more difficult when subject areas were presumed to be not only the means but the ends of education.

That same year, William Kilpatrick (1918) published his popular paper, "The Project Method." In it he called for a move away from coercive teaching and passive learning toward engagement of children in purposeful projects, using a problem-solving method, through which they would achieve an array of academic, social, and ethical learnings. As a result, Kilpatrick claimed, the child "would emerge with a higher degree of skill and knowledge and his learning will longer abide with him" (p. 326). But more than this, he argued that the type of project he proposed was "the typical unit of the worthy life in a democratic society, [and] so also should be made the typical unit of school procedure" (p. 323). Though not using the term *integration*, Kilpatrick had thus alluded to what would become the basic grounds for curriculum integration as a design theory: personal and social/democratic learning brought together with the problem-centered project as a context for organizing and integrating knowledge.

While Kilpatrick and others at Teachers College, Columbia University, drew major attention in the movement away from a passive, subject-centered curriculum, they were not the only ones advocating for that cause. In 1920, Junius Meriam published *Child Life and the Curriculum*, a classic and comprehensive treatise on the progressive elementary school. Among other ideas, he rejected both the simple correlation of the Herbartians and the "final integration" of the social efficiency advocates. Instead, he called for organization of the curriculum around life activities and problems as organizing centers, an arrangement he called "initial integration" (p. 251). Thus by the 1920s the concept of integration was ready to surface as a central idea in the emerging progressive education movement.

FROM INTEGRATION TO CORE CURRICULUM

As these events were taking place, a teacher by the name of Meredith Smith was in the midst of a five-year classroom "experiment" at the University of Pittsburgh's School of Childhood. Having studied at the National Kindergarten College[1] and at Columbia University, Smith was inspired by John Dewey's theory of experience, according to which interactions with the environment constitute a continuous process of learning. To try out this theory, Smith (1921) engaged a group of young children, starting in first grade, in a "community project." The children began by building small houses for themselves and then brought them together as a community. Smith then gave the children small dolls to represent people in their "community." Deciding that they wanted and needed to have a "real" community, one that included caring for the needs of children, the students took on various social and occupational roles, interacted about their relationships in each, and otherwise created what Smith took to be a model, realistic community. Over time, as the community became more elaborate, the children became interested in sophisticated social and economic issues, including those beyond their immediate setting.

In the end, Smith made several claims about this kind of education. First, by following their own sense of what needed to be done in forming a community, rather than simply being told, the children more effectively learned the variety of tasks and relationships involved. Second, in reaching out to others to form a community, the children presumably experienced the meaning of democracy and learned how to act accordingly. Third, in the context of these experiences, content and skills were not only willingly learned but sought out as they were needed. As she put it:

> Thus, in the work and play connected with the community project, children are identifying themselves with the world of human endeavor, with its arts and sciences, its industries and social institutions; and ideals of right and justice are being instilled in their minds. Reading, writing, and number work become the means by which they may more efficiently carry out their purposes. Introduced into situations which involve its use, children appreciate the meaning and significance of certain knowledge, and as the need for skill increases, they become interested in the drill that is essential to acquisition of that knowledge. (M. Smith, 1921, p. 304)

There were many accounts at the time of "experiments" with the project method, especially after publication of Kilpatrick's paper. Smith's report might simply have been one more among these except that she then undertook doctoral studies at Teachers College in an "attempt to find a psychological basis for the method employed" (M. Smith, 1927, p. v). What she found, no doubt with direction from Kilpatrick, was organismic psychology. Rejecting traditional stimulus-response theories of behavior, organismic psychologists claimed that organisms were not only affected by their environment but, in turn, acted upon it so that both were continuously changing one another. Whereas lower organic forms simply underwent physical change in this process, humankind actually gained increasing control over the environment and used it for creative expression. Presumably this was true not only for humankind as a whole, but also for individuals. It was here that Smith staked her basic claim, that in this account of the exchange between organism and the environment was "the psychological explanation of what is involved in experience as Dewey analyzes it" (M. Smith, 1927, p. 8).

On this basis, Smith concluded that traditional education in which children were simply told about the knowledge and experience of humankind was wrong, since it placed children in a passive role and denied their capacity to act on their environment. Instead, she proposed guiding children (as in her own project) to engage in purposeful activities by which they would learn from acting on their environment in increasingly sophisticated ways. Thus content and skills would not be "ends in themselves . . . [but] means to the attainment of consequences desired, to the realization of purpose" (M. Smith, 1927, p. 84). When such purposeful activity would take place in groups, "the acquisition of skill, knowledge, and power on the part of the individual then become a social asset" (p. 84) leading toward a "point of realization of cooperative relations, of a truly democratic attitude" (p. 67).

If there had been anything like a "ribbon-cutting" event for the idea of curriculum integration, this was it. In organismic psychology, the term for the process of growth, development, and change resulting from interaction with the environment was *integration*. It was this term that Smith used to describe not only the individual growth of children in her project but also the convergence of individuals in a democratic community. Hence the title of Smith's 1927 doctoral dissertation: *Education and the Integration of Behavior*.

Smith served as principal of several progressive schools in California and wrote little in succeeding years, but the idea of integration, as she had framed it, gained popularity among many progressive educators. For example, in 1926 Kilpatrick had referred to integration solely in the social sense of growing interdependence among people. Seven years later, writing in a book edited by Kilpatrick, Childs and Dewey (1933) spoke of the need to integrate cultural and material values "with the purposes of the common life" and to "promote integration of the individual" (p. 66). In the same volume, Hullfish (1933) called for a curriculum organized around problems of social integration that would become increasingly sophisticated across the school years. As an example, Hullfish described a possible classroom project on community development similar to Smith's project with the children in Pittsburgh. And in 1936, Kilpatrick reiterated this expanded meaning of integration by referring not only to social integration but to the "integration of learning results" (p. 71).

In 1931, the National Education Association's convention featured no less than 19 separate papers on integration as it related to topics from psychology to community participation (e.g., Cadman, 1931). That same year, the NEA Department of Superintendence yearbook featured a paper entitled "Principles of Integration" (Hopkins & Armentrout, 1931) in which the co-authors claimed that educational integration involved two considerations, "(1) the nature of the individual, and (2) the social function of the school" (p. 367). At a time when the idea of integration was in increasing danger of being tied only to the child-centered activity movement, this was an extremely important reminder that the school was also charged with social integration and that individual integration involved interactions in a social environment. The paper was also important inasmuch as one of its co-authors, L. Thomas Hopkins, a Professor at Teachers College, Columbia University, and a curriculum specialist at its Lincoln School, was to become the major theorist of and spokesperson for integration in the curriculum.

Throughout the 1930s the idea of integration was the subject of considerable discussion and experimentation. Books, journal articles, and convention speeches addressed a variety of pertinent topics: the need to emphasize social as well as personal integration (DeBoer, 1936; Dix, 1936); research favoring integration over the separate-subject approach in both elementary and secondary schools (Oberholtzer, 1934, 1937; Wrightstone, 1935, 1936, 1938); the relationship between personal-social integration and democracy (Cary, 1937; Rugg, 1936, 1939); clarification of terminology (Hatfield, 1935; Curriculum Commission of the National Council of Teachers of English, 1935); and accounts of curriculum integration in schools (Daniel, 1932; Sweeney, Barry, & Schoelkopf, 1932; Dix, 1936; Oberholtzer, 1937). By 1936 the frequency of journal articles about "integration" reached such a point that the term was given its own category in the Education Index.

It was Hopkins, though, who was at the center of the movement for integration in the curriculum and who persistently sounded its major themes. In a foreword to Sweeney and colleagues' 1932 book describing a unit on cultures, Hopkins defined the "integrated" type of curriculum as "organized around the immediate, abiding interests and assured future needs of the learner, utilizing materials selected from all areas of the social heritage regardless of subject division" (p. viii). Here, as in other articles (Hopkins & Armentrout, 1931; Hopkins, 1935), he took into account both personal and social integration while suggesting that the integration of knowledge was a key to helping young people achieve both. This theme was expanded in the 1937 volume *Integration: Its Meaning and Application*, which brought together papers authored by specialists in philosophy, sociology, psychology, and biology under the editorship of Hopkins. In his 1941 work, *Interaction: The Democratic Process*, Hopkins emphasized the social context of integration, calling for a problem- and experience-centered curriculum collaboratively planned by teachers and students, an idea that he had consistently emphasized as a crucial aspect of meaningful education (Hopkins, 1929). It was here, as well, that he criticized the increasingly inappropriate use of the term *integration* to describe curriculum projects that actually involved multidisciplinary, broad fields and other organizations that were rooted in subject-matter mastery rather than personal and social integration.

By the early 1940s, the attention of the curriculum field was focused on the Eight Year Study, a major undertaking of the Progressive Education Association. In the study, graduates of high schools that experimented with various nonseparate-subject curriculum forms outperformed graduates of traditional programs on academic and social measures of success in college (Aikin, 1942). Moreover, graduates of the six high schools that moved most dramatically away from the separate-subject approach and in the direction of curriculum integration showed the largest advantage over graduates of traditional separate-subject programs. Certainly the more urgent considerations of World War II contributed to the somewhat lackluster reception of what is now considered a landmark study in curriculum. But in the long run, it is at least as likely that the study's limited impact was foreshadowed early on by a principal of one of the 30 experimental schools. Describing the possibility of changing the separate-subject curriculum, even with a guarantee that graduates would be accepted to college, she said this: "My teachers and I do not know what to do with this freedom. It challenges and frightens us. I fear that we have come to love our chains" (Aikin, 1942, p. 16).

While use of the term *integration* declined somewhat in the 1940s, its major concepts appeared in various designs that had been evolving for three decades. At the elementary school level, for example, one such design was the activity curriculum, a child-centered concept that mixed developmentalism, organismic psychology, and the project approach. Another was the so-called experience curriculum, which aimed to use the experiences of young people as a source of curriculum possibilities, as a bridge to the larger world, and as a context for bringing external knowledge to them. Others, such as the "persistent-life-situations" approach (Stratemeyer, Forkner, McKim, & Passow, 1947), attempted to cover both the elementary and secondary schools.

Another reform topic was clarification of sources for organizing the curriculum, a topic that was in the foreground of the curriculum field for more than three decades after the Eight Year Study. In this case, the concepts of integration were especially pronounced in approaches based on "major social issues" and "emerging needs" of young people. As distinguished from the separate-subject approach and the broad-fields or correlated approach, the first two sounded the themes of personal and social integration, integration of knowledge, and problem-solving experiences (Rugg, 1936; Wesley, 1941).

But nowhere was the idea of integration more evident than in the "core" programs that emerged from the Eight Year Study and found their way into junior and senior high schools as a way of organizing the general education requirements for secondary schools (Corey et al., 1942; Macdonald, 1971). While the implementation of the "core" concept was often limited to subject correlations, its leading advocates called for a problem-centered approach collaboratively planned by teachers and students without regard for subject-area divisions (Wright, 1950; Faunce & Bossing, 1951; Lurry & Alberty, 1957; Alberty & Alberty, 1962). Moreover, the teachers and students were to work in a multiperiod block of time and, in some cases, even stay together over two or more years (Zapf, 1959).

Arguing now not just for a curriculum design, but for the very character of the school curriculum, advocates of curriculum integration carried the concept into the progressive "core" curriculum movement. Indeed, in many ways, the latter became the umbrella program for the various aspects of the integration concept. Using students' experiences and concerns promoted personal integration and offered the secondary school version of the more elementary-based experience curriculum. The focus on social problems, especially those drawn from the local community, offered a direct approach to social integration, often expressed as sharply as the social reconstructionists had envisioned it. The use of "pupil–teacher planning" was not only a method of identifying student concerns but a major device for bringing democracy to the classroom. The integration of knowledge through projects and other activities led to meaningful learning, the application of skills, and the integration of experiences. And in the end, by bringing all of these ideas together, advocates of "core" programs offered a comprehensive and practical program for general education (Faunce & Bossing, 1951; Burton, 1952; Hopkins, 1955; Hock & Hill, 1960).

Though block-time programs using non-separate-subject approaches in general were used in almost 50% of junior and senior high schools, those of the problem-centered type were less common (Wright, 1950, 1958). But at the junior and senior high levels, these programs are probably as close as schools have come to curriculum integration on a scale larger than the bold efforts of individuals or small groups of teachers in isolated pockets within traditional schools. In retrospect, these were the salad days of curriculum integration.

TROUBLE IN PARADISE

The demise of curriculum approaches and arrangements such as core and experience-centered programs is often attributed to the launching of the Russian satellite *Sputnik* in 1957 and the subsequent emphasis on technical subjects and the structure of disciplines in the decade that followed. However, progressive curriculum approaches were already under attack from right-wing critics by the mid-1940s and continued to be a favorite target through the McCarthy era of the 1950s. Typical accusations that progressive education was the work of communists and was the cause of juvenile delinquency were thin cover for deeper fears of powerful conservatives that young people might learn to analyze the weaknesses of social institutions and economic practices (Brameld, 1944).

Moreover, the classical humanists had once again gone on the attack with their own rhetoric of high-culture elitism. According to one, Mortimer Smith (1949), the alleged demise of intellectualism was due to "opposition to logically organized subject matter . . . [and] building the curriculum around major 'goals' or 'objectives' and integrating all subject matter around these goals" (p. 44). As a result, he pointed out, "the old saw about the little boy from the modern school who countered his mother's complaint about his getting only 30 in arithmetic and spelling by proudly pointing out that he got 100 in Postwar Planning, is not without a large kernel of truth" (p. 45). The suggested remedy, of course, was a good dose of a curriculum driven by and organized around the traditional school subjects.

The force with which that position was articulated in the 1950s by Arthur Bestor (1953) and others would have done high-culture traditionalists in any time proud. Its virulence was rivaled only by the combination of anti-communism and social efficiency in the verbal bombshells of Admiral Hyman Rickover (1959) and other post-*Sputnik* critics of education. Taken together, these two forces were clearly too much for advocates of progressive curriculum approaches. Without much resistance, the disciplines of knowledge were put back on the pedestal they had enjoyed before 1918.

Ironically, though, four works appeared in the middle of all of this that directly addressed the topic of integration in the curriculum. The first was a summary done by Paul Hanna and Arch Lang in the 1950 edition of the *Encyclopedia of Educational Research*. After discussing background and various approaches related to integration, they laid out 19 characteristics of an integrative school. More important than the list of items, however, was the way in which they were integrated by the authors to sound the central themes of integration:

> I. If the school is to lead in the task of integrating our value system, then it will identify and transmit cultural values, make human welfare central in identifying values, foster cross-cultural contacts, provide for growth in social thinking, [and] lead pupils to take responsible part in civic agencies.
>
> II. If the school is to serve the local and the larger community in fostering integration, then it will act as a community center, maintain strong link-

ages with the larger community, make itself liked as well as approved, foster cross-cultural contacts, promote humanitarian activities, provide for the development of varied kinds of social competence and especially integrative leadership, plan systematically for common learnings, foster cooperative effort, [and] exemplify democratic methods of action.

III. If the school is to provide an environment favorable to the integration of the individual personality, then it will provide nurture for each child's physical and psychic needs, foster attitudes of affection and harmony, bring children under the guidance of well-adjusted people, provide for varied patterns of development, teach through first-hand learning, teach through purposeful activity, foster responsible planning, provide for personal growth through cooperative effort, provide for growth through responsible civic participation, facilitate the development of adult status, [and] plan for continuity of development. (pp. 596–598)

The second work directly addressing integration was the culminating volume in the long line of work on integration carried out by L. Thomas Hopkins, *The Emerging Self in School and Home* (1954). Here Hopkins reiterated his belief in the relationship between creative individuality and a democratic society, and argued once more for the so-called experience approach to curriculum. The third work was the 57th Yearbook of the National Society for the Study of Education, entitled *The Integration of Educational Experiences* (N. B. Henry, 1958), a compendium of ideas that in many ways replicated the 1937 volume edited by Hopkins. Writing in the opening chapter, Paul Dressel spoke for the other authors in saying that "we hope to replace a mystifying mosaic of many separated courses and unrelated extra-curriculum experiences by an educational program which has unity in the eyes of most students" (p. 23).

The fourth work was a small volume entitled *The Curriculum Integration Concept Applied in the Elementary School* (Ward, Suttle, & Otto, 1960). The main purpose of this volume was to report case studies of two attempts to implement curriculum integration programs. While these studies were most instructive, especially in the distinctions made between multidisciplinary and integrated approaches, the more important contribution was in the early chapters, where the authors offered an extensive review of the theory and history of the integration concept.

Ironically, while the 1960s were a period of social ferment in many areas of life, curriculum reform was not one of them. In fact, quite the opposite—the main story of the decade emphasized the separate subjects through the "structure-of-the-disciplines" movement, triggered by Jerome Bruner's *The Process of Education* (1960) and funded mainly by the National Science Foundation. This and the related efforts to systematize instruction through performance objectives, packaged programs, and curriculum

management systems were hardly a context for the flexibility and democratic planning associated with curriculum integration.

By the 1970s, talk about integration in the United States had basically
died down, as had work on the various curriculum designs into which its
principles had been integrated, except as items for historical review (e.g.,
Bellack & Kliebard, 1971; Macdonald, 1971). The term *integration* was
dropped as a heading from the Education Index as of the July–December,
1974, edition and was hardly mentioned in U.S. educational literature for
more than a decade, except for rare occasions like the curriculum texts by
Tanner and Tanner (1980) and Schubert (1986) or Meeth's (1978) reference to integration as an advanced form of interdisciplinary curriculum.
And despite continuing efforts by groups like the National Association for
Core Curriculum, as well as a few individuals (Vars, 1969; Beane, 1975;
Lounsbury & Vars, 1978; Beane, 1980), general education and even the
term *core* itself were almost never defined in any way except as a collec-
tion of required subjects.

Meanwhile sociological work on the politics of knowledge in Great
Britain and elsewhere offered analyses of curriculum integration that were,
if anything, more sophisticated than those typically done during the hey-
day of integration talk in the United States (Ingram, 1979). Michael Young
(1971) and Bernstein (1975), for example, explored the implications of
dissolving subject boundaries and opening up the curriculum to everyday
knowledge as those concepts related to academic and class politics inside
and outside the school. Hirst and Peters (1970), advocates of a discipline-
centered curriculum, took up the question of the relation of curriculum
integration to particular purposes that varied from the separate-subject
approach. And Gleeson and Whitty (1976) described efforts to transform
social studies from a fragmented collection of social sciences to an integrated field that was problem-centered and collaboratively planned.

Though the stage was being set in the 1980s for a new episode of explicit work on curriculum integration, the curriculum field itself had largely
turned its attention away from issues of design and toward analysis of
cultural and economic politics in curriculum content and decision making. In the face of a great conservative restoration, that kind of political
analysis was extremely important. However, as talk heated up about a
national curriculum and tests, objections were raised almost only with
regard to who would get to define the content. The fact that the curriculum and tests were to be based on a strict separate-subject approach was
basically unchallenged, even though that approach had long been regarded
as one of the ways in which the dominant culture silenced the voices of
the nonprivileged. What two decades earlier would have been a chorus of

objections to the exclusive emphasis on separate subjects was now only a few marginalized voices.

LOST AND FOUND

In the 1990s, there has been a new round of interest in integration in the curriculum. Two aspects of this current interest stand out in relation to the historical background of curriculum integration. One is that while the period of conservative ascendancy of the 1950s basically shut down the previous era of integration efforts, the present efforts are actually emerging in the midst of conservatism. The other noteworthy aspect is that while the present round of work shares considerable similarities with the earlier round, there are also striking differences between the two.

The stage for the current round of interest was set by curriculum developments that built momentum in the 1980s. Early childhood educators forcefully reiterated their longstanding support of integration in the curriculum for young children (Bredekamp, 1987). Advocates of whole-language approaches in the elementary school began to call for an expansion of their work to encompass areas other than language arts (Pearson, 1989; Hiebert & Fisher, 1990; Routman, 1991; Zemelman, Daniels, & Hyde, 1993). Multidisciplinary units and projects, which had mixed support in middle schools for two decades, were given a boost by national and state reports recommending they be used more frequently. Science educators pushed for a social-problems approach in science–technology–society programs (Yager, 1988). Educators who had promoted the use of multidisciplinary approaches in "gifted-and-talented" programs began to work in the larger arena of general education. And advocates of "Outcomes-Based Education" argued with some success that a separate-subject approach would be insufficient in pursuing sophisticated levels of learning.

The contemporary equivalent of the earlier organismic psychology argument, that integration arises from some basic human inclination or need, has come from two claims. The first claim, made by Caine and Caine (1991) and based on their summary of research on the brain (especially that of Hart [1983]), is that because the brain seeks patterns by which to "integrate" information, the curriculum ought to be organized around integrative themes and projects. The second claim, made by multisource and constructivist learning theorists, is that new ideas and skills are most likely internalized and carried forward when they are encountered in relation to previous experience, meaningful contexts, and whole ideas rather than when they are taught as abstract, fragmented parts (e.g., Iran-Nejad et al., 1990; Brooks & Brooks, 1993). To the extent that these and similar claims have been used to advance the idea of integration in the curriculum by Kovalik (1994) and others, this focus on the "organic" is quite similar to the effect of Smith and Kilpatrick's work in the 1920s and 1930s.

Though curriculum theorists (e.g., Vars, 1987; Harter & Gehrke, 1989; Beane, 1990a, 1990b; Miller, Cassie, & Drake, 1990; Gehrke, 1991) had begun to look again at the idea of integration and its implications for curriculum organization by the late 1980s, the use of the term in relation to curriculum was given momentum by two widely distributed publications. One was the 1989 volume *Interdisciplinary Curriculum: Design and Implementation*, edited by Heidi Hayes Jacobs and distributed to tens of thousands of members of the Association for Supervision and Curriculum Development. The other was a paper by Betty Shoemaker (1991), "Education 2000: Integrated Curriculum," in which she described efforts in Eugene, Oregon, to create thematic units at the elementary school level. Curiously, though, Jacobs, who had previously written about interdisciplinary curriculum in gifted education (Jacobs & Borland, 1986), tied integration not to the line of work described in this chapter but to the so-called "integrated day" that was part of the British Infant School movement in the 1960s and "most commonly seen in the United States in preschools and kindergarten programs" (Jacobs, 1989, p. 17). As I noted earlier, however, the integrated day structure did not necessarily involve integration in the curriculum. But the mere presence of the term in such a widely distributed work was a crucial factor in bringing it back into common usage.

Among the similarities to the earlier movement is the ambiguous use of terms such as *integration* and *integrated* to cover almost any arrangement beyond the separate-subject approach. In 1941, Hopkins observed that, "In some instances the same word, such as integrated, coordinated, or core, is used to designate a type of curriculum near the subject and also near the experience end of the scale" (p. 19). A scan of journals, conference programs, and school-based project reports clearly suggests the same is true today, especially with regard to confusion over the differences between multidisciplinary approaches and curriculum integration, as well as the sources of organizing centers for the curriculum.

This is perhaps not surprising given that the term *integration* has been applied to a range of approaches that are really multidisciplinary and interdisciplinary, and thus subject-based (e.g., Fogarty, 1991; Jacobs, 1989; Krogh, 1990; Meeth, 1978). In that sense, the historical concept of curriculum integration is sometimes more accurately represented in approaches called "transdisciplinary" (Drake, 1993; Meeth, 1978) or "supradisciplinary" (Brady, 1995) in which an attempt is made to use real-world issues as organizing centers without regard for subject-area lines.

The misplacement of curriculum integration within a collection of interdisciplinary approaches is even more problematic when such a collection is portrayed as a continuum, thus implying that teachers moving out of the separate-subject approach might first go to a mutidisciplinary one and then to integration. This might make some sense if curriculum integration was merely another way to arrange subject-area content. We have seen, however, that curriculum integration involves a very different way of thinking about curriculum than discipline-based approaches, including its theory of the organization and uses of knowledge. As Krug (1957) pointed out in distinguishing the subject and broad-fields approaches from the problems and experience organizations, "The four points in this classification . . . do not form a continuous scale. One cannot assume that normal 'progress' in curriculum planning consists of moving steadily from one point in this classification to another" (p. 107).

That observation suggests a major difference between much of the work labeled "integration" today and that of the earlier period, namely, the absence of any connection to the broader topic of curriculum design theory. Indeed, there is general neglect of this topic within the field of curriculum studies itself. But in the more popular arena of school reform, it probably has more to do with the tendency to see curriculum integration only as a technique rather than as part of a comprehensive, progressive educational philosophy. This is the case with many "school-to-work" projects following the SCANS (1992) report as well as many associated with the well-known "dimensions of learning" program (Marzano, Pickering, & Brandt, 1990).

Clearly, though, the most striking difference between the current round of interest and the earlier one is the consistent failure in popular literature, journals, and conference programs to tie curriculum integration to broader social purposes. Instead, the idea of "integration" is focused almost only on individual learning and is more often associated with units on teddy bears, aviation, and the Middle Ages than with substantive issues and topics such as conflict, the environment, or the future. It would perhaps be understandable if this lack of social consciousness were clearly due to conservative pressures in our times. But the lack of historical references in popular discourse around curriculum integration suggests a less thoughtful reason, namely, that people don't know there is a history behind this work and that it was meant to involve the social purposes of democracy.

This does not mean that the idea of democratic social integration is completely ignored in current work. In fact, that connection has been made quite explicit in several places (Beane, 1990b, 1993a, 1995a; Wraga, 1991; Wood, 1992; Zemelman, Daniels, & Hyde, 1993; Apple & Beane, 1995;

Cross, 1995; Pate, Homestead, & McGinnis, 1996). Moreover, a few authors (Tanner, 1989; Vars, 1991, 1993) have published brief historical
overviews of integrative curriculum, while others (Gehrke, 1991; Martinello & Cook, 1994; Wraga, 1993; Beane, 1995b) have taken pains to
reference historical antecedents. Nevertheless, these sources have not
found their way into school deliberations nearly as often as some of the
less well grounded texts and programs mentioned earlier.

On the other hand, as the current round of interest has evolved, a
promising possibility for reclaiming the deeper meaning of curriculum
integration in schools is emerging, just as it did 70 years ago. I refer here
to the rich collection of accounts of various kinds of integration projects
written by teachers and administrators (e.g., Stevenson & Carr, 1993;
Brazee & Capelluti, 1995; Brodhagen, 1995; Pace, 1995; Siu-Runyan & Faircloth, 1995; Alexander, 1995; Nagel, 1996; Pate, Homestead, & McGinnis,
1996). The growing number of these kinds of accounts suggests that two
very important things are happening. First, many teachers and administrators have not been constrained by the narrow understanding of integration. And, second, the broader meaning of integration is not merely a
rhetorical flourish.

But because the social-democratic aspect has too often been left out
of popular conversations about integration, the curriculum philosophy it
involves is almost entirely absent from debates over what ought to be involved in general education. So it is, without much resistance, that talk
about common school experiences or a core curriculum focuses only on
the matter of whose list of facts and skills will be included on which high-
stakes national and state tests that will continue to verify who is privileged
and who is not among our children. And the matter of curriculum integration is reduced to a side debate over how well those bloated lists of facts
and skills will still be covered in this or that multidisciplinary approach.

Meanwhile, there is silence about the possibility of a curriculum for
personal and social integration that has space for more than high-culture
knowledge, that engages the aspirations and concerns of young people,
and that uses knowledge for important social purposes. In the end, the
absence of such ideas from most (mistaken) explanations of curriculum
integration has helped make it possible to reintroduce the approach during the current conservative restoration. As we shall see later, however,
where those progressive ideas have begun to work their way back into
the conversation, curriculum integration has come under attack, just as it
did 50 years ago.

Clearly, an important history has generally been ignored in the renewed attention to curriculum integration, a history that could inform
current work in important ways. I do not mean to say that the early his-

tory gives us all we need to know; work on the politics of curriculum in the past two decades responds to many of the crucial mistakes and omissions of that earlier time. But as I said at the outset of this chapter, given the long line of work described in the historical sketch in this chapter and the difficult work of teachers and others to make that history happen, it is hard not to feel angry when contemporary educators say that curriculum integration is "like what we did in the 1960s," or "what they did at Summerhill" (which they didn't), or, as I heard a presenter at a conference say, "interdisciplinary, integration, multidisciplinary—all those terms mean the same thing." Sometimes you wonder.

NOTE

1. The National Kindergarten College became the National College of Education and is now a part of National–Louis University.

CHAPTER 3

Curriculum Integration and the Disciplines of Knowledge

At a conference on curriculum integration, a speaker who admitted only recent introduction to the concept said, "From a quick look at various readings, it seems that the disciplines of knowledge are the enemy of curriculum integration." Unwittingly or not, that statement went to the very heart of perhaps the most contentious issue in current conversations about curriculum integration. Simply put, the issue is this: If we move away from the subject-centered approach to curriculum organization, will the disciplines of knowledge be abandoned or lost in the shuffle? As an advocate for curriculum integration, I want to set the record straight. In *thoughtful* pursuit of authentic curriculum integration, the disciplines of knowledge are not the enemy. Instead they are a useful and necessary ally.

Remember that defining curriculum integration in the first chapter required frequent reference to "knowledge." How could there not be? Broadening and deepening understandings about ourselves and our world requires that we come to know "stuff," and to do that we must be skilled in ways of knowing and understanding. As it turns out, the disciplines of knowledge include a great deal (but not all) of what we know about ourselves and our world, ways of making meaning and of communicating those meanings. Thus authentic curriculum integration, involving as it does the search for self and social meaning, must take the disciplines of knowledge seriously. Again, though, it is about more than just the correlation of knowledge from various disciplines or cleverly rearranging lesson plans.

WHAT IS THE PROBLEM?

Theoretically defining the relations between curriculum integration and the disciplines of knowledge is that easy. But pointing out that the two are not mutually exclusive does not resolve the tension over how those relations work in the practical context of curriculum integration. Part of the reason is that the problem is not with the disciplines of knowledge themselves, but with their representation in the separate-subject approach to the curriculum. Put another way, the issue is not whether the disciplines of knowledge are useful, but how they might appropriately be brought into the lives of young people. And more than that, do they include all that is known or that might be of use in the search for self and social meaning?

A discipline of knowledge is a field of inquiry about some aspect of the world—the physical world, the flow of events over time, numeric structures, and so on. A discipline of knowledge offers a lens through which to view the world—a specialized set of techniques or processes by which to interpret or explain various phenomena. Beyond that, a discipline also provides a sense of community for people with a shared, special interest as they seek to stretch the limits of what is already known in that discipline. Those on the front edges of a discipline know that disciplinary boundaries are fluid and often connect with other disciplines to create interdisciplinary fields and projects (Klein, 1990).

Though school-based subject areas, like disciplines of knowledge, partition knowledge into differentiated categories, they are not the same thing as disciplines. Some subjects, such as history or mathematics, come close, but they are really institutionally based representations of disciplines, since they deal with a boundaried selection of what is already known within them. That selection is based upon what someone believes ought to be known (or is not worth knowing) about some discipline by (young) people who do not work within it or are unfamiliar with its progress to date. Other subjects, such as biology or algebra or home economics, are subsets of disciplines and are boundaried in even more specialized ways. And still other subjects, such as career education or foreign languages, may lay far-reaching claims of connection to some discipline, but their presence in schools really has to do with economic, social, or academic aspirations.

In this sense, a discipline of knowledge and its representative school subject area are not the same thing, even though they may be concerned with similar bodies of knowledge. They serve quite different purposes, offer quite different experiences for those who encounter them, and have quite different notions about the fluidity of boundaries that presumably set one area of inquiry off from others. These differences are substantial enough that the identification of a school subject area as, for example, "history" amounts to an appropriation of the name attached to its corresponding discipline of knowledge. Subject areas are, in the end, a more severe case of "hardening of the categories" than the disciplines they supposedly represent.

This distinction is not made to demean the work of subject teachers or to relegate them to a status below disciplinary scholars. Rather, the distinction is made to point out that calling for an end to the separate-subject approach to school curriculum organization is not at all to reject or abandon the disciplines of knowledge. But in saying this, I want to quickly warn that such a claim does not simply open the door to a renewal of Essentialist conversations about the "structure of disciplines" or their "teachability" that Bruner (1960) and others (Ford & Pugno, 1964; King & Brownell, 1966; Alpern, 1967) encouraged in the past and that are now revisited in lists of national and state content standards. Packaged in these ways, the separate-subject approach may be all dressed up, but it still has no place to go.

It is worth noting that Bruner himself apparently recognized this risk when, 10 years after publication of *The Process of Education*, he reconsidered its place in educational policy. Having just spoken of poverty, racism, injustice, and dispossession, Bruner (1971) said this:

> I believe I would be quite satisfied to declare, if not a moratorium, then something of a de-emphasis on matters that have to do with the structure of history, the structure of physics, the nature of mathematical consistency, and deal with curriculum rather in the context of the problems that face us. We might better concern ourselves with how those problems can be solved, not just by practical action, but by putting knowledge, wherever we find it and in whatever form we find it, to work in these massive tasks. We might put vocation and intention back into the process of education, much more firmly than we had it there before. (pp. 29–30)

It is from just this kind of thinking that the case for curriculum integration emerges. Creating a curriculum for and with young people begins with an examination of the problems, issues, and concerns of life as it is being lived in a real world. Organizing centers or themes are drawn from that examination. To work through such themes, to broaden and deepen our understanding of ourselves and our world, and to communicate those meanings, we must necessarily draw upon the disciplines of knowledge. Again, therein lies a great deal of what we know about ourselves and our world, ways in which we might explore them further, and possibilities for communicating meanings. Our reach for help in this kind of curriculum is a purposeful and directed activity—we do not simply identify questions and concerns and then sit around and wait for enlightenment to come to us. Instead, we intentionally and contextually "put knowledge to work."

INSIDE THE SUBJECT APPROACH

More and more educators are coming to realize that there is a fundamental tension in schools that current restructuring proposals are simply not addressing, no matter how radical their rhetoric might otherwise be. That tension has to do with the curriculum that mediates the relationships among teachers and young people. After all, teachers and their students do not come together on a random or voluntary social basis—they do not meet casually and decide to "do school." Instead, they are brought together to do something—namely, the curriculum—and if that curriculum is wrought with fundamental problems, then the relationships among teachers and students will almost certainly be strained.

Advocates of curriculum integration, myself included, locate a large measure of that tension in the continuing organization of the planned curriculum around separate subject areas. For that reason, systematic critiques of the separate-subject approach have been made over many decades (e.g., Rugg, 1936; Hopkins, 1941; Brady, 1989; Beane, 1993a; Connell, 1993). Here, I touch upon the major points of contention in order to clarify the claims made earlier in this chapter.

First, the separate-subject approach, as a selective representation of disciplines of knowledge, has incorrectly portrayed the latter as "ends" rather than "means" of education (Dewey, 1900/1915; Henry, 1956; Brady, 1995). Young people, and adults, have been led to believe that the purpose of education is to master or "collect" (Bernstein, 1975) facts, principles, and skills that have been selected for inclusion in one or another subject area instead of learning how those might be used to inform larger real-life purposes. Nowhere is this more apparent than in the way that young people are introduced to disciplines of knowledge through the subject approach itself, most often by being made to memorize specialized vocabulary or subskills rather than learning what each discipline is really about and what its interests are.

Second, we have been getting signals since the 1930s that the separate-subject approach is not necessarily the only, or even the most appropriate, route to those purposes that its own advocates claim for their approach (Wrightstone, 1935, 1936; Informal Committee of the Progressive Education Association, 1941; Aikin, 1942; F. C. Jenkins, 1947; P. Hanna & Lang, 1950; Mickelson, 1957; Alberty, 1960, Wright, 1958; Vars, 1996). As these research reviews have indicated, young people tend to do at least as well, and often better, on traditional measures of academic achievement and adjustment to further education as the curriculum moves further in the direction of integration. Moreover, with regard to other kinds of achievement, especially interpersonal understanding and relations, the separate-subject approach appears to be significantly less successful than arrangements based on the concept of integration.

Third, the separate subjects, and the disciplines of knowledge they are meant to represent, are territories carved out by academicians for their own interests and purposes. Imposed on schools, the subject approach thus suggests that the "good life" is defined as intellectual activity within narrowly defined areas (e.g., Bloom, 1987; Hirsch, 1987). The implication that this is the only version of a "good life" or the best one or even a widely desirable one demeans the lives of so many others outside the academy who have quite different views and aspirations.

The fact that those academicians who so narrowly define the "good life" in this way happen to be mostly white, upper middle class, and male means that the knowledge they prize and endorse is of a particular kind. Such knowledge, of course, is the cultural heritage of their limited group, and thus the cultures of "other" people have been marginalized in the separate-subject approach. This is why the traditional question of the curriculum field—"What knowledge is of most worth?"—has been amended with another—"Whose knowledge is of most worth?" As Michael Apple (1990) has pointed out, "one major reason that the subject-centered curricula dominate most schools, that integrated curricula are found in relatively few schools, is at least partly the result of the place of the school in maximizing the production of high status knowledge" (p. 38).

Pressing this point a bit further, we can see how such knowledge works on behalf of privileged young people in whose culture it is regularly found while working harshly against those from nonprivileged homes and nondominant cultures. In this way, the separate-subject approach and its selective content plays more than a small role in the "sort and select" system that has been an unbecoming feature of our schools for so long. While curriculum integration by itself cannot resolve this issue, the use of real-life themes demands a wider range of content, while the placement of that content in thematic contexts is likely to make it more accessible for young people (Macdonald, 1971; Iran-Nejad et al., 1990).

For most young people, including those who are privileged, the separate-subject approach offers little more than a disconnected and incoherent assortment of facts and skills. There is no unity, no real sense to it all. It is as if in real life, when faced with problems or puzzling situations, we stop to ask which part is science, which part mathematics, which part art, and so on. We are taken aback when young people ask, "Why are we doing this?" And our responses—"because it will be on the test" or "Because you will need it next year"—are hardly sufficient answers to that question, let alone justification for placing anything in the curriculum.

The deadening effect the separate-subject approach has on the lives of young people cannot be overestimated. In too many places, they are still taught how to diagram complex sentences as if that was the key to the writing process, still made to memorize the names and routes of European explorers, still taught the same arithmetic year after year, page after page, with no particular connection to their lives. I believe such irrelevance has also had a deadening effect on the lives of many teachers. Had they known that this would be their routine for 30 years or more and that high tension would result, many would have imagined other lines of work to be far more attractive. And who could blame them?

The separate-subject approach carries the legacy of Western-style classical humanism that views the world in divided compartments. This view was shored up in the last century by the theories of faculty psychology and mental discipline that described the mind as a compartmentalized "muscle" whose parts were to be exercised separately by particular disciplines (Kliebard, 1984). The reasoning faculty, for example, was supposedly exercised by the "objective logic" of mathematics, with the assumption that such reasoning would then be applied to any new situations, including social ones.

Though faculty psychology and mental discipline were discredited by the turn of the century, both live on in some interpretations of split-brain and multiple-intelligence theories. And suspect as it has now become, classical humanism still looms large in curriculum organization as part of the "official knowledge" to which Apple (1993) refers.

In constructing such a critique we must remember Dewey's admonition (1938) that any nondominant idea about education (in this case, curriculum integration) must not be defended solely on grounds of rejection of another (in this case, the inadequacy of the separate-subject approach). Curriculum integration does not just mean doing the same things differently but rather doing something different. It has its own theories of purpose, knowledge, and learning and is able to stand on those without the necessity of standing on the corpse of the separate-subject approach. However, the subject-centered approach is so rooted in the deep structures and folklore of schooling that its critique is virtually necessary to even raise the possibility of other approaches (M. F. D. Young, 1971). It is almost as if it had been conceived supernaturally instead of constructed by real people with particular values and beliefs (Williams, 1961; Goodson, 1985).

KNOWLEDGE IN AN INTEGRATIVE CURRICULUM

Having exposed the shortcomings of the separate-subject approach, we may now turn back to the more optimistic relations between the disciplines of knowledge and curriculum integration. How does knowledge look in the context of curriculum integration? What happens to the disciplines of knowledge? How are they used?

In practice, curriculum integration begins with the identification of organizing centers for learning experiences. As previously noted, the themes are drawn from life concerns, as, for example, "Conflict," "Living in the Future," "Cultures and Identities," "Jobs, Money, Careers," or "The Environment." In some cases the themes are identified by teachers, while in the most sophisticated instances they emerge from collaborative planning with young people (Zapf, 1959; Noar, 1966; Beane, 1991, 1992; Brodhagen, Weilbacher, & Beane, 1992; Brodhagen, 1995). Planning then proceeds directly to creating activities to address the theme and related issues. There is no intermediate step in which attempts are made to identify what various subject areas might contribute to the theme.

As noted in Chapter 1, this is a very important distinction, since curriculum integration, in theory and practice, transcends subject-area and disciplinary identifications with an eye toward integrative activities that use knowledge without regard for subject or discipline lines. Other approaches, such as the multidisciplinary or interdisciplinary ones, may not follow a strict subject-centered format, but they nevertheless retain subject-area and disciplinary distinctions around some more or less unifying theme (James, 1972; Bernstein, 1975; Jacobs, 1989). In curriculum integration, the disciplines of knowledge come into play as resources from which to draw in the context of the theme and related issues and activities.

Recall the examples with which I began Chapter 1. In a unit on "The Environment," students might create simulations of different biomes with real and constructed artifacts and offer guided "tours" of their work. Or they might experiment with the effects of polluted substances on plant growth. Or they might set up and manage a recycling program in the classroom or school. Or they might identify the raw products in various clothing items and investigate where they come from, find out who makes them, and analyze environmental and economic impacts of the entire process. Or they might identify environmental problems in their local community and seek ways to resolve them.

In the unit on "Living in the Future" described in Chapter 1, recall that young people might be engaged in activities such as conducting a survey of peer beliefs about the future, tabulating the results, and preparing summary reports. Or they might use technological, recreational, entertainment, or social-trend data to extrapolate forecasts or scenarios on probable futures for one or more areas. Or they might check the accuracy of past forecasts to see if they actually occurred. Or they might recommend population, health, recreation, transportation, and conservation policies for the future of their community. Or they might imagine how they might look when they are older by studying the effects of aging on facial features.

I have used the word *or* between activities since an integrative unit may involve use of any number or more of these. But the point is this: Any careful reading of the activities should reveal that if they are done thoughtfully, they would draw heavily upon a variety of disciplines of knowledge for facts, skills, concepts, and understandings.

For example, in constructing surveys, tabulating data, and preparing reports, one would need to draw heavily from social sciences, language arts, and mathematics. Suppose that some young people did not know how to compute percentages or make graphs. Obviously the teacher(s) would help them to learn how to do these things or, if necessary, find someone who could. In experimenting with effects of pollutants on plant life, some young people might not know how to carry out controlled tests. In that case, someone would teach them how to do that. Does this mean that schools would intentionally employ teachers who know "stuff" from disciplines of knowledge? Certainly! But in curriculum integration, teachers work first as generalists on integrative themes and secondarily as content specialists.

Note that in curriculum integration, knowledge from the disciplines is repositioned into the context of the theme, questions, and activities at hand. Even when teaching and learning move into what looks like discipline-based instruction, they are always done explicitly in the context of the theme and for a reason driven by it. It is here that knowledge comes to life, here where it has meaning, and here where it is more likely to be "learned." Particular knowledge is not abstracted or fragmented, as is the case when its identity and purpose are tied only to its place within a discipline of knowledge or school subject area.

Repositioning knowledge in this way raises two issues that cannot be ignored. First, subject-area sequences that have previously defined the flow of knowledge tend to be rearranged in curriculum integration, since knowledge is called forth when pertinent rather than when convenient. While this is upsetting to some subject-loyal teachers, we should note the irony that sequences often vary from school to school and state to state. In other words, sequences are more arbitrary than those who construct and defend them would have us believe. The fact that even some subject-area associations have moved away from traditional notions of sequencing should tell us something. In the end, though, advocates of curriculum integration are more interested in the rhythms and patterns of inquiring young minds than the scopes and sequences of subject-area specialists. The work done within the context of curriculum integration *is* a curriculum; there is not another "curriculum" waiting in the wings to be taught.

Second, it is entirely possible, even probable, that not all of the information and skills presently disseminated by separate-subject teaching will come to the surface in the context of curriculum integration. But let's face it, there is a good deal of trivia presently being disseminated in schools that would only be necessary or meaningful if and when one actually became a specialist in one or another discipline of knowledge, and even then some of it would probably be on shaky ground. In some places, the separate-subject curriculum looks more like preparation for *The New York Times* crossword puzzle than for specialization in a discipline. Besides, the very idea of knowing all that "stuff" is a pipe dream in an era of knowledge explosion when so many of yesterday's "truths" seem to dissolve in the high tide of today's new knowledge.

Curriculum integration, on the other hand, calls forth those ideas that are most important and powerful in the disciplines of knowledge—the ones that are most significant because they emerge in life itself. And because they are placed in the context of personally and socially significant concerns, they are more likely to have real meaning in the lives of young people, the kind of meaning they do not have now.

As boundaries disappear, curriculum integration is also likely to engage knowledge that ordinarily falls between the cracks of disciplines and subject areas. This is particularly the case as knowledge is applied to problematic situations. For example, in exploring the influences of media, young people might investigate what the word *average* means in the context of the presumed consumer interests of the "average person." What does *average* mean here? How is "average" arrived at when used this way? How can mathematics be used to manipulate meanings?

Certainly this kind of knowledge is being attended to by some scholars who work in disciplines of knowledge (and their work is an important resource for those who advocate curriculum integration). But can the same be said for those who live within the boundaries of school subject areas? Isn't it also the case that those discipline-based scholars have to move beyond the boundaries of their home disciplines in order to work on such matters? And if this is so, why is it that they feel the need to do so when so many other people are adamant about leaving those same boundaries intact in schools?

Critics of curriculum integration love to convey their deep concern that it will destroy the integrity of the disciplines of knowledge. I am puzzled by this. What possible integrity could there be for any kind of knowledge apart from how it connects with other forms to help us investigate and understand the problems, concerns, and issues that confront us in the real world? Furthermore, what kind of integrity is it that the disciplines of knowledge now have in the minds of young people? Am I missing something here? Or is it the case that "integrity" is really a code for "subject boundaries" and "dominant-culture knowledge?"

As a last chance, some critics also suggest that perhaps curriculum integration would be a good idea—but only after a thorough grounding in the separate subjects. If we were talking about house building, the foundation metaphor might work well. However, in the case of learning, it is the "whole" context that gives particular knowledge meaning and accessibility (Iran-Nejad et al., 1990). Besides, if we have to wait for the kind of foundation that such critics mean, we will probably never see any integration—just like now.

BEYOND THE DEBATE

Despite the matter-of-fact tone I have used here, it would be a mistake to believe that the understanding and practice of curriculum integration is clear of confusion. The widespread assumption that curriculum integration ignores knowledge from the traditional disciplines is itself evidence that advocates of curriculum integration have not necessarily been clear in their criticisms of the separate-subject approach or their delineations of the difference between school subjects and disciplines of knowledge.

Moreover, having established the link between curriculum integration and the disciplines of knowledge, many questions remain. For example, are some kinds of knowledge more likely than others to emerge in the context of life-centered themes? Are some themes more likely than others to serve well as contexts for integrating wide ranges of knowledge? What size chunk of life should an integrative theme encompass? How can we be certain that integrated knowledge helps young people continuously expand meanings rather than simply accumulating without meaning, as is usually the case in the separate-subject approach (Bellack, 1956)?

Curriculum integration is a distinctive and progressive approach to curriculum organization and the uses of knowledge. Yet it does not reject outright or abandon all that has been of concern from other views of schooling. This is especially apparent with regard to the disciplines of knowledge that are necessarily drawn upon in responsible curriculum integration. This point is not a matter of compromise but of common sense. Advocates of curriculum integration may criticize the separate-subject approach and its implied purpose of schooling, they may rebel at the narcissism of subject-area loyalists, and they may decry the deadening effects of the separate-subject curriculum. But they do not intend to walk away from knowledge, and for that reason, the disciplines of knowledge are clearly not the "enemy" of curriculum integration.

CHAPTER 4

In the Place of High Pedagogy

In the past several years, I have spent considerable time with teachers who have been working with a particular curriculum design that uses the concept of curriculum integration in its broadest sense. While in the classrooms of some of them, there have been many moments when I could not help but marvel at what the students were involved with: doing exciting projects, doing presentations with apparent ease and confidence, articulating what they were learning and what it was about, and more. On one occasion, a friend of mine was along visiting for a day and noted that what he saw was unusual in comparison to other classrooms that he had visited. He said, "This is real learning."

Sometimes when people are struck by the high quality of an experience or event or object, they say, "Now that's the real thing." The saying is common enough that it can even be used in commercials. The "real thing" might be an artistic masterpiece, an intensely exciting contest, a breathtaking physical maneuver, or a dazzling meal. Whatever it is, the "real thing" is at once extraordinary and authentic. It is also what we always hope will happen but don't necessarily expect to. The "real thing" is unmistakably first-rate. In curriculum and teaching, it is what I have seen many times in those classrooms in the past several years. As my friend said, it's "real learning."

In this chapter I draw heavily on the work of those teachers, including what I have experienced teaching with some of them, what I have observed in their classrooms, what they have told me, and what they have written. Too numerous to name, they are elementary, middle, and high school teachers throughout the United States, Canada, and Australia.

The curriculum design many of these teachers use is shown in Figure 4.1. The curriculum involved in this design is based on themes that are found at the intersection of personal concerns of young people and larger world concerns. So, for example, a theme such as "Health and Diseases" might emerge from questions about personal health and longevity, along with questions about whether cures will be found for life-threatening diseases and whether air, land, and water pollution will increase. A theme such

Figure 4.1   A Design for Curriculum Integration

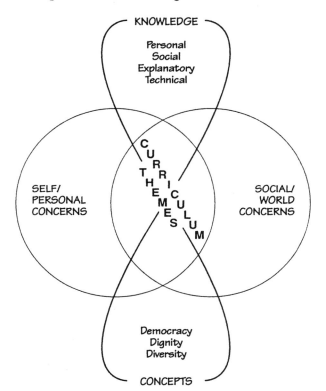

as "Living in the Future" may emerge from concerns about personal futures and about the future of the larger world. A theme such as "Conflict" might emerge from concerns about family and neighborhood crime and violence along with concerns about global violence and terrorism. Continuing with the design, four kinds of knowledge are then integrated as young people are engaged in work focused on the themes and related concerns:

- *Personal knowledge*—addressing self concerns and ways of knowing about self.
- *Social knowledge*—addressing social and world issues, from peer to gobal relationships, and ways of critically examining these.
- *Explanatory knowledge*—content that names, describes, explains, and interprets, including that involved in the disciplines of knowledge as well as commonsense or "popular" knowledge.

- *Technical knowledge*—ways of investigating, communicating, analyzing, and expressing, including many of the skills already promoted in schools.

Finally, democratic values, respect for human dignity, and prizing of diversity are to be emphasized in all curriculum experiences (Beane, 1990a).

This design was intended to bring together the various aspects of curriculum integration—personal integration of experiences, social integration, integration of knowledge, and an integrative design—as well as concepts such as democratic education (Beane, 1990b, 1993a). For example, the use of personal concerns as one source of organizing themes is likely to enhance possibilities for personal integration. Using social issues as another source provides a context for encouraging social integration while also opening such issues for critical, democratic examination. Using themes that link personal and social issues promotes the integration of self and social interest, a marker of social responsibility in a democratic society. Such themes also offer a personally and socially significant context for the integration of knowledge.

In a sense, then, the design serves as an idealized version of curriculum integration. The obvious question is, "How might we bring such a design to life in the classroom?" It is this question that I want to explore by describing some of the practices that seem to be emerging from the classrooms of those teachers I have worked or visited with. The practices, along with the professional commitment and talent of the teachers, are what help to make these classrooms places of high pedagogy.

COLLABORATIVE PLANNING

As discussed in Chapter 1, the idea of planning with young people is very important in creating an integrative curriculum. Connecting new experiences to previous ones and personally contextualizing knowledge must sooner or later involve direct participation by young people themselves. Moreover, bringing democracy to life in the classroom requires that students have a genuine say in the curriculum and that their say count for something.

There are many ways in which young people might be involved in planning their curriculum. For example, teachers might survey students to determine questions and concerns that suggest themes. Or they might select a problem-centered theme and then involve students in identifying questions and related activities within the theme. Such was the case of a ninth-grade teacher whose invitation to suggest questions for a unit on cultures drew 300 responses. On the other hand, a first-grade teacher developed a year-long environmental studies project based on one student's question about where the garbage in the school dumpster went after the dumpster was full.

However, many teachers who use the curriculum design described earlier engage young people in a collaborative planning process that involves two questions: "What questions or concerns do you have about yourself?" and "What questions or concerns do you have about the world?" After students write their questions individually, small groups are formed to find questions that are shared by individuals within the group, such as the following:

Self Questions

How long will I live?
What will I look like when I am older?
Do other people think I am the way I think I am?
What job will I have?
What would I do if I met an extraterrestrial?
Will I ever go to outer space?
Why do I fight with my brother and sister?
Should I get a tattoo?
Will I be poor and homeless?
Will my family still be there when I am older?
Will my parents accept me as an adult?
Where will I live when I am older?
Will I get married and have children?
Why do I act the way I do?
Why do I have to go to school?
Will I have the same friends when I am older?
Why do I look the way I do?
Will I go to college?
Will I be like my parents?

World Questions

Will we ever live in outer space?
What will happen to the earth in the future?
Why are there so many crimes?
Why do people hate each other?
Will racism ever end?
Will there ever be a president who is not a white man?
Are there other planets than the ones we know about?

Who owns outer space?
Will the United States ever be out of debt?
Will cures be found for cancer and AIDS?
Where does garbage go?
Who will win the next election?
Why are schools the way they are?
Will the rain forests be saved?
Why is there so much prejudice?
What is the purpose of time?
How do you know when something is real?
Will drug dealing stop?
What will people evolve to look like?
Will hoverboards replace skateboards?
Is time travel possible?
How many kinds of species are there?
Why are there so many poor people?

The group then tries to identify organizing centers or themes that use both self and world questions, such as the following sample themes:

Jobs, Money, Careers
Living in the Future
Environmental Problems
Conflict and Violence
Mysteries, Beliefs, Illusions, Superstitions
"ISMS" and Prejudice
Government and Politics
Drugs, Diseases, Health
Cultures
Lifestyles of the Rich and Famous . . . and Not!
Outer Space

Once the whole group has reached consensus on a list of themes, a vote is held to see which one will be undertaken first. As illustrated in Figures 4.2–4.4, relevant questions for any given theme are then selected from all the small-group lists, and the group brainstorms ideas about possible activities they might do to seek answers to their questions. Once a final plan is made, the unit gets underway. As each unit is completed, the group chooses its next theme from the original list, reviews the questions they used to create it, and makes a plan for the new unit.

This kind of collaborative planning addresses integration in ways that other kinds do not. First, the curriculum is created, quite literally, from the bottom up: out of the questions and concerns of young people themselves. Chances are thus greatly increased that knowledge and activities will be contextualized as nearly as possible to the students' own prior experience. Second, as activities are collaboratively identified, students have an opportunity to indicate how they think they might best approach knowledge and experience. Third, as the process moves from individual to group questions and from personal to larger world concerns, students have direct experience with the integration of self and social interests.

However, collaborative planning is not without tensions. One tension involves the continuing question of whether young people reveal their "true" selves in classrooms, given the complexities of gender, race, class, and other sources of power dynamics within a group (Orner, 1992). Moreover, many young people are suspicious of invitations to plan with teachers because experience tells them that teachers may not welcome their ideas or that some teachers create the illusion of democracy by "engineering consent" to predetermined plans (Graebner, 1988). And, finally, there are always some students who for one reason or another cannot think of anything to add to the group's planning and are thus carried along without signaling their consent. Teachers who try to do genuine planning with students usually make efforts to counter these issues by first building a sense of community and trust. Even so, ever-present tension in group dynamics makes such planning less glamorous than typical participation theory implies.

A second tension in the kind of planning I have described arises from the belief that it is based on whimsical interests of young people. Now it may be that an integrative curriculum is more interesting and engaging for young people. But the planning itself is based on questions and concerns about self and world, two areas in which people are unlikely to name trivial issues. Current fads find a place within themes that involve popular culture, but the themes are about substantive topics and issues, not the fads themselves. Curriculum integration is issue-centered in its organization, not interest-centered. The teachers don't ask what the students are "interested" in or "want to study," but what they are concerned about.

Still another tension involves the constant challenges from people who question the significance and legitimacy of the questions and activities students suggest and the knowledge those activities engage. Teachers who engage in serious curriculum integration of the kind I am describing fully understand their professional obligation to bring certain kinds of knowledge and experience to young people, including much of what is included in state and district mandates. This is why, in addition to the two questions about self and world concerns, a third question is always on the teachers' minds: What questions or concerns does the world pose to young

Figure 4.2 Living in the Future Unit: Concept Web, Sample Questions, and Sample Activities

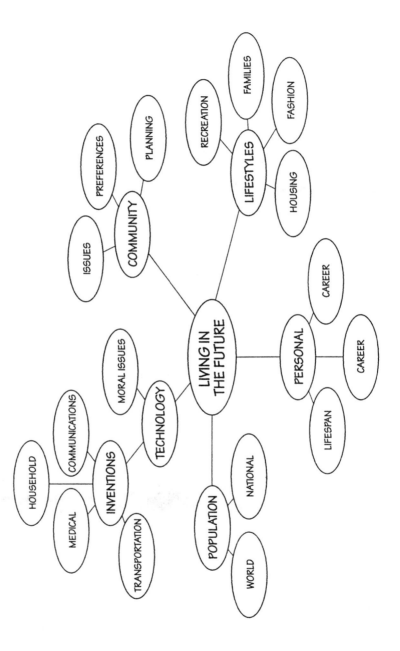

Figure 4.2 (continued) Sample Questions

- How long will I live?
- What will I look like in the future?
- Will I be healthy?
- Will I achieve my goals?
- Will I make enough money to support myself?
- Will I ever be in a life or death situation?
- Will I end up doing the same things my parents are doing?
- How will my kids turn out (school, drugs, etc.)?
- Will I break my bad habits?
- Will I move to another state/country?
- Will I go to college?
- How much is the world going to change?
- Will we ever have a president who is not a white man?
- Will cures be found for cancer and AIDS?
- Will we live underwater or on another planet?
- What new inventions will be made?

Figure 4.2 (continued) Sample Activities

- Develop recommendations for our city in the year 2020 in areas such as land use, transportation, education, resource conservation, government, and health care.
- Make a time capsule with predictions for self and world.
- Plan a reunion for our group in the year 2015.
- Find past forecasts for our times; research to find out if they were accurate and why the forecasters believed they might happen.
- Find out how popular technologies (e.g. computers, VCR's, cars) were invented.
- Create models of inventions for the future.
- Do personal timelines and extend them into the future.
- Investigate work and education requirements related to personal goals.
- Hold a debate on the pros and cons of new technologies.
- Develop a family health history to determine average lifespans and genetic health factors.
- Use makeup or computer imaging to see what we might look like when we are older.
- Research options to prevent or delay aging, such as exercise, cosmetic surgery, and medical technology.
- Make our own forecasts and survey students at other schools for theirs. Do a research report comparing the two.

Figure 4.3 Conflict and Violence Unit: Concept Web, Sample Questions, and Sample Activities

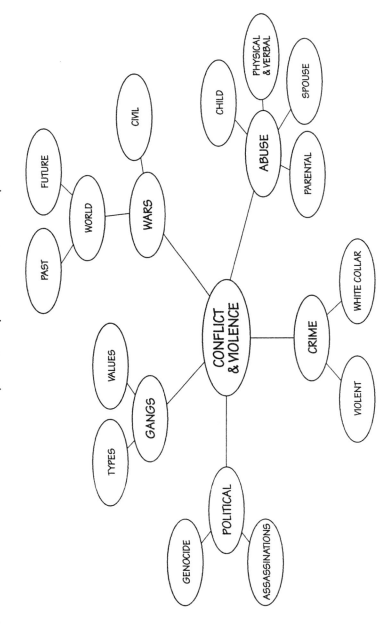

Figure 4.3 (continued) Sample Questions

• When will gang violence stop?
• Will there ever be world peace?
• What happens in death camps?
• When will abuse stop?
• Who shot J.F.K. and Martin Luther King, Jr.?
• Will we win the "war" on illegal drugs?
• Will there ever be enough for all to survive?
• Why do people hurt/kill each other?
• Will I ever go to prison?
• Will I ever be kidnapped?
• When/How will the world end?

Figure 4.3 (continued) Sample Activities

• Interview gang members to find out why they belong to a gang.
• Research reasons given for killing and determine what would have to happen to stop it.
• Interview someone who was in a death camp.
• Find out where death camps are today and research why they exist.
• Research rates and causes of different kinds of abuse.
• Write a story about how the world might end.
• Using newspapers and magazines for information, place flag pins on a large-scale world map in places where there are wars or other kinds of major conflicts going on.
• Research local trend statistics on various types of crime and make forecasts about future problems and solutions.

57

Figure 4.4 Money Unit: Concept Web, Sample Questions, and Sample Activities

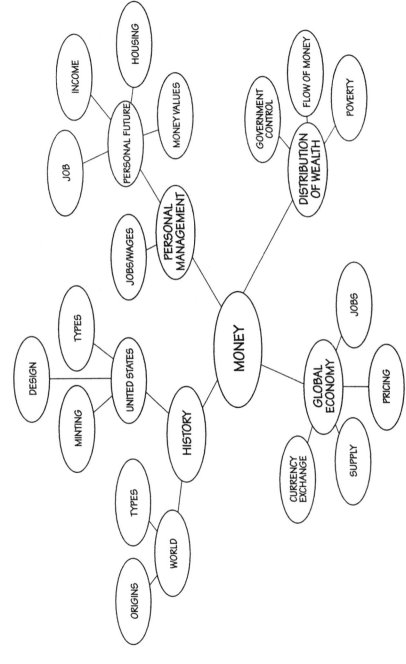

Figure 4.4 (continued) Sample Questions

- When and why was money invented?
- What is the largest denomination in the world?
- Why are presidents on U.S. bills?
- Where and how does U.S. money get made?
- How often and for what reasons has the U.S. changed its money?
- What happens to old money?
- Will money always exist?
- How do currency exchanges work?
- What is the most expensive item in the world?
- How are prices set?
- Who controls the most money in the U.S?
- Will there ever be a time when no one is poor?
- Will I have enough money when I am older?
- What is a minimum wage job?
- What jobs bring more income?
- Will there ever be no homeless people?
- Will I be greedy?
- Will I own a big house?

Figure 4.4 (continued) Sample Activities

- Identify some favorite fashion items (clothes, sneakers, etc.) and research where they are from, what resources were used in making them, wages of workers who made them, and who benefits from profits on them.
- Interview local merchants about how prices are set for various kinds of merchandise that they sell.
- Using selections from television, music, and movies, compare value messages about money, wealth, and poverty.
- Debate issues related to wage and wealth distribution, such as the gap between working-class wages and those paid to business executives and professional athletes.
- Create a timeline on the evolution of money as a system of exchange.
- Create a classroom economy system and analyze patterns of wealth distribution over several weeks.
- Invite a guest speaker to explain how global economic connections work and how they influence national and local economies.
- Visit a local bank to learn about personal money management topics such as loans, different types of accounts, and so on.
- Interview people from other countries about the economy and currency systems in their countries.
- Design and display new forms of currency that might be used in the U.S.
- Find out how wealth is distributed in the U.S. and how that has changed over time. Forecast what might happen in the future.
- Write a future autobiography that demonstrates occupation, personal lifestyle, and money values.

people that they might not see or know about? So, for example, if a group of students did not identify concerns around cultural diversity, the teacher, understanding this as a crucial social issue, would introduce it into the planning process. On the other hand, young people live in the same world that adults do and are more than a little aware of significant issues in that world. Moreover, they care about those issues and want to learn more about them.

These three tensions taken together correctly suggest that teachers who use curriculum integration are constantly faced with the question of how much guidance to give students in their work. Faced with obligations to help young people to do their own "integrating," to bring participatory democracy to life, and to attend to external mandates, this is a continuing and unavoidable question. As we shall see in this and the next chapter, it is only one of the tensions for teachers in the place of high pedagogy.

Sometimes, though, young people themselves reduce the tension considerably. When I first sketched out the curriculum design around self and social/world concerns, I had envisioned asking students for the self part while drawing the world part from the list of obvious issues, such as conflict, cultures, futures, the environment, and so on. However, as we began to plan with young people, we asked them to name questions and concerns about the world along with their self questions. As the examples cited earlier indicate, the young people named almost all of the same issues we teachers would have. I was not really surprised by this, only a little embarrassed that I had momentarily forgotten that young people, too, have experience in the world.

PERFORMING KNOWLEDGE

Toward the end of a unit on environmental issues, a group of students decided they wanted to divide into five subgroups to create five large-scale biomes in their classroom. In working out evaluative criteria for the projects, the teachers and students agreed that each subgroup would need to be able to do a "museum-style" tour of their biome: presenting information, answering questions, and so on. As part of their preparation, the whole group went on a fieldtrip to a science museum. Much to the surprise of their tour guide, the students had many questions about how to conduct a tour, how to guess what questions might be asked, how to decide what to say, and how to arrange displays. The tour guide admitted to never having been asked questions like these before.

No particular approach to curriculum has a monopoly on the use of activities that simultaneously draw knowledge from two or more disciplines. Even separate-subject teachers sometimes introduce knowledge from outside their given subject area. For teachers who advocate curriculum integration, however, such activities are the daily fare of classroom life. But nothing is as apt to signal curriculum integration as the use of large, whole-group projects that integrate all aspects of a unit.

Picture, for example, a unit entitled "Living in the Future" that culminates with students presenting recommendations to a city planning official regarding what they believe their city ought to be like in the year 2020 in areas such as land use, transportation, government, social services, and so on. Picture a unit on "Environmental Issues" that culminates with students presenting the results of a school "conservation audit." Picture a unit "Politics and Prejudice" that culminates with student recommendations regarding cultural diversity in textbooks and other school resources. Imagine as well that in each case, students have participated in the initial identification of the culminating activity and worked on it throughout the unit while also engaging in various other large-group, small-group, and individual activities related to the theme.

Large projects of these kinds touch virtually every dimension of integration. Individuals have the opportunity to create their own integrating contexts and methods through participation in planning the projects. The projects are large enough to allow integration of a wide array of knowledge. Being problem-centered, they also involve using knowledge to work on socially significant issues. And since they involve social action, the projects encourage integration of students' in-school and out-of-school concerns and experiences. The fact that the projects are complex means that there is space for diverse learning styles, interests, skill levels, modes of expression, and so on. As these individual matters are brought together in the group project, the idea of social integration is brought to life.

Advocates of curriculum integration are often asked how they manage assessment of student learning. Along with the obvious observations, unit tests (usually consisting of the unit questions), portfolios, and other typical devices, these large projects serve as important venues for both teachers and students to gather information about what content and skills have been learned within a unit. (It is worth noting as well that in keeping with the collaborative mode of working, students and teachers usually work together to establish methods and related criteria for assessing learning. In addition, assessment results typically involve both student self-evaluation and student-led parent/guardian conferences.)

Since students present, demonstrate, and exhibit their work for the group, knowledge is not simply something individuals accumulate for themselves. Rather it is put to use for the *group's* further understanding of the problem or issue around which the unit is organized. It is in these moments when young people "perform knowledge" that we are able to see in action the simultaneous workings of personal and social integration. As Carol Smith, a teacher who has used this approach for many years, told me, "There is surely something compelling about having your work 'count' for something bigger than a grade at unit's end."

ORGANIZING AND USING KNOWLEDGE

By definition, classrooms where curriculum integration is used are marked by the organization and uses of knowledge that I detailed in earlier chapters and in the above description of integrating projects. Inside those classrooms, however, even more about integrating knowledge is revealed.

When the curriculum is opened to issues in the larger world and especially when the questions and concerns of young people help shape the curriculum, the content and interests of popular culture are suddenly placed alongside those of the "high culture" that has traditionally dominated the curriculum. For example, a unit on "Conflict and Violence" may be driven as much by tabloid accounts of assassination conspiracy as by concerns over how wars are started. A unit on "Outer Space" may likewise emerge from questions about black holes *and* rumors about "visits" from extraterrestrials.

While high-culture and popular-culture interests are in conflict elsewhere, teachers who use curriculum integration see both as sources of knowledge in their classrooms. Popular culture is, after all, the preferred culture of large numbers of people, including many of the young people the teachers work with. To reject popular culture would thus inhibit the possibilities of connecting with students' personal experiences, while rejecting high culture would deprive nonprivileged students access to knowledge that they might not encounter outside the school but still be expected to know. But those teachers also understand that both sources of knowledge are open to critical inquiry, since both are socially constructed and neither has a monopoly on "the truth."

Along those same lines, a premium is placed on the democratic uses of knowledge. One of these, already discussed, is the use of knowledge to address social problems and issues. Another is the critical analysis of knowledge and knowledge sources, as in the case of a teacher who engaged students in an analysis of various school textbooks using the criterion of cultural diversity. A third is the underlying idea that the problem-centered themes for the curriculum are created out of the personal and social experiences of students and their teachers rather than the subject-centered interests favored by distant academics and bureaucrats.

Related to that third point is the unspoken understanding that as young people and their teachers respond to their own questions and concerns, they are constructing their own meanings. In this case, the right to define what counts as worthwhile knowledge is not left entirely in the hands of academics and bureaucrats. While external knowledge is a very important source of ideas from which to draw, it is not the only source of meaning, nor is it necessarily taken for granted that it is always the most reliable one. It is important to note, however, that this kind of "constructivism" is way beyond some mainstream versions that simply involve young people in finding their own way to predefined answers to questions within one or another subject area.

Since the integration of knowledge is often an unfamiliar curriculum feature for many students and parents, however, teachers who use curriculum integration usually work hard to show how what Apple (1993) calls "official knowledge" is still present and accounted for. One way they do this is through frequent "process" meetings with students in which the group identifies and discusses the content and skills that are being used at any given time. Another is to show parents a list of content and skills for each unit broken out into subject categories. Yet another is through the use of portfolios that are the centerpiece of student-led parent conferences (Brodhagen, 1994, 1995). Another is to invite parents to spend time in the classroom, to view student projects and presentations, and to serve as resource persons for various topics. Still another is to make use of traditional resources, such as textbooks, in cases where they are useful for information gathering. All of this is, of course, in addition to the long trail of evidence mentioned in the last chapter showing that students involved in curriculum integration do at least as well as or better on standard knowledge tests than cohorts who are involved in separate-subject arrangements.

However, success with that kind of knowledge is only the beginning of what curriculum integration is about. If it were only about that, the complexity and conflict involved in carrying out curriculum integration in schools that are organized for a separate-subject approach could hardly be justified. As implied in the description of integrating projects and the democratic uses of knowledge, young people involved in curriculum integration are more likely to be engaged with much richer, more sophisticated, and more complex knowledges than those who are confined within the boundaries of separate subjects: critical and creative thinking, valuing, constructing meanings, problem solving, and social action. As such skills reach the surface of the curriculum, as young people perform their knowledge, as knowledge is instrumentally applied to significant issues, we finally see, in these classrooms, a demonstration of the old slogan, "Knowledge is power." And unlike the traditional subject curriculum, that power has to do with working on important social issues rather than getting ready for academic "trivial pursuit."

Too often teachers working with curriculum integration are put on the defensive when it comes to how knowledge is organized and used in their classrooms. They end up explaining research evidence, test results, how they often use direct teaching for particular skills, and so on. A few, though not enough, have hit on a more powerful response to critics: Longer lists of fragmented, subject-based content and skill do not make for higher standards or a more challenging curriculum, nor do they make knowledge more accessible for young people. Instead, they argue, emphasis on real issues, contextual learning, problem solving, thinking, critical inquiry, and so on does make for higher standards, for a more challenging curriculum, and for broader access to knowledge. As we shall see in the next chapter, some critics do understand this about curriculum integration, namely, those who reject the approach precisely because they fear that too many children will know too much.

A few years ago, I was working with a group of teachers in a summer school setting where the students who were enrolled had failed two or more subjects during the year. Clearly this was a group of young people who were down on their luck academically. After planning with the students, the teachers had set up an arrangement of small-group meetings to investigate various issues and large-group meetings for processing common research criteria, journaling, discussing emerging research findings, and so on. About a week into the summer school, some visitors came from a nearby college and observed the students working in the library gathering information for their projects. They also talked with some students about what they were doing and how their work was organized. As the visitors were leaving the building, they remarked to the principal that this was a really exciting program and that the students seemed to be doing very well in their work. Then they asked if there was also a remedial summer program in the school for students who had had academic trouble during the year. Some curriculum arrangements hide what young people can do. Other curriculum arrangements open the way for them.

CREATING COMMUNITIES

On a few occasions I have been able to interview students who have spent one year doing real curriculum integration work and then moved back into a traditional separate-subject arrangement the next year. Although I try to ask them about what they think they gained or lost in relation to their present classmates who were in a separate-subject program the year before, they want to talk about how the two approaches compare and what they miss the most. Mostly they miss the give-and-take of the group, working together on the big projects, and having serious group discussions. They name this as "missing the sense of community."

Among other purposes, curriculum integration is intended to promote social integration. For this reason teachers who use the approach make concerted efforts to create democratic communities within their classrooms. The sense of community is built not only on the relationships among the adults and young people but on the idea that they are mutually engaged in addressing shared questions and concerns. In these ways, young people have an opportunity to learn through experience the social knowledge that is part of the democratic way of life.

Teachers who use curriculum integration at this level spend time engaged in explicit activities aimed at community building (e.g., M. Smith, 1927; Zapf, 1959; Brodhagen, 1995; Alexander, 1995; Pate, Homestead, & McGinnis, 1996). For example, governance of the community often begins with writing a class "constitution" or otherwise deciding the ground rules for the group's time together. World maps are used to illustrate ethnic backgrounds, and local maps to show where individuals live in relation to the school. Students create surveys to find out interests, attitudes, and preferences, and then make charts and graphs to create a statistical portrait of the group. Autobiographies are written so that individuals can reflect on how they do or don't fit the group portrait. None of these are contrived "sensitivity" gimmicks. Rather, they are meant as serious attempts to bring the concept of an organic, democratic community to life.

As groups plan their curriculum together, the issue of integrating self and social interest becomes a serious concern. The framework for the planning described earlier is based upon the idea of general rather than specialized, individualistic education. It is meant to bring young people together in a shared experience of mutual concern rather than to deal with independent interests of each individual. There is, of course, plenty of room for individual interests within the project-based format, but even then, individual projects are tied to and shared as part of larger group projects. This is perhaps best observed in those moments when the group works to find consensus among individual questions in order to forge a single set of themes for the whole group.

Beyond those curriculum matters, teachers who use curriculum integration also seem to consistently value working with diverse groups of young people. For example, their classroom groups often incorporate special education students (and their teachers) as part of inclusion projects. This interest comes not only from a philosophic commitment to diversity but confidence that a collaboratively planned, project-centered curriculum will have plenty of room for diverse ideas and diverse routes to achievement. In fact, visitors to these classrooms are often caught off guard when they learn that students whom they have watched give substantive presentations are among those classified in the special education population. As we will see later, however, a general education that brings diverse young people together in the name of democracy is not always easy to maintain, especially in an era when so many parents demand that the curriculum be differentiated for their own child.

The notion of creating a community also emerges from the theory of classroom management that seems consistent among teachers who use curriculum integration. For example, steering committees are often formed to help manage various units. The whole group takes on questions about criteria for assessing student work and for evaluating aspects of the curriculum. The group also tries to work out conflicts among members by using whatever rules they made at the beginning of the year, while teachers make every effort to keep students who have behavior problems in the group rather than in the principal's office.

Ironically, these efforts often complicate teachers' lives when some administrators mistake this theory of curriculum for a theory of discipline and the teachers find their classrooms disproportionately populated by students whom other teachers in the school simply do not want to work with. The intensity of such situations, to say nothing of their unfairness, tests the emotional energy of even the most committed teachers. Yet they almost always persist because the matter of social integration is as much a part of the curriculum as the content of various units. And difficult as things may be, there are rewarding moments.

One of the groups we worked with included a girl who was identified by the school as "emotionally disturbed" and for that reason was usually in a classroom with one or two similarly labeled peers and one or two special education teachers. Sometime after we had completed our planning and worked well into our first unit, we were joined by the principal of the school. Curious to hear from the students about what they were doing, he asked a number of questions about integration of knowledge, collaborative planning, and project work, which they answered in turn. As he was preparing to close the discussion, the girl who was labeled "emotionally disturbed" raised her hand. Called upon, she stood up in front of the group and said this to the principal: "I am usually put in a room by myself with a teacher because people think I'm nobody. But since I've been here working with all these other people, I've been happy. When I'm here, I feel like I am somebody."

RELATIONSHIPS

As part of workshops on curriculum integration, I often show a video of teachers and students planning the curriculum in the way described earlier (Wisconsin Public Telecommunications for Education, 1992). It is a very powerful video, and I always look forward to seeing it again. However, on one occasion a few years ago, I instead watched the teachers in the workshop as they viewed the video. Watching them, I suddenly realized that it was not so much the curriculum design that captured their attention but the relationships that the teachers on the video had with their students. Sure enough, when I asked about this, several workshop participants told me that they wished their students "looked at them like that" or "talked to them like that." They said they would be willing to try the curriculum design if that would happen for them.

Teachers and students are brought together because they are supposed to do "something." That something is the curriculum. If the curriculum is somehow unsettling, then it is very likely that the relations between teachers and students will be strained. Surely an abstract, fragmented, incoherent curriculum would do just that. Curriculum integration, on the other hand, opens up the possibility for more positive relationships.

To begin with, teachers who choose to use curriculum integration have already made several commitments that create fundamental shifts in traditional teacher–student relationships:

- To share curriculum and other decision making with young people
- To focus more on the concerns of young people than on predetermined "scope-and-sequence" content guides
- To take on questions to which they do not know the answers and, therefore, to learn along with students
- To take seriously meanings constructed by students
- To advocate for young peoples' right to have this kind of curriculum

In making these commitments, teachers demonstrate their desire to shift power relations in classrooms. For example, one rule of thumb we often used from the beginning in our classroom work was this: If there is something we want to know, we go ask the students. Teachers who think like this are immediately placed in a less adversarial position with students regarding both management and curriculum. Together with attempts at community building, these shifts in power suggest much deeper commitments to student engagement than simply using flashy activities.

Relationships with young people are not the only ones these teachers seem to seek. Because textbooks and other typical school resources are usually silent on self and social issues, teachers who use curriculum integration cultivate networks of resource people who can bring specialized knowledge to their classrooms. They also find unusual ways to bring parents and other significant adults in young peoples' lives into the curriculum—as resources for projects, through family events at school, and, in a few cases, through some level of participation in helping define social/world issues for the curriculum. And since relationships work both ways, the teachers also seek to make the community a site for study, service projects, and social action in the curriculum.

But in the end, it is the relationships with students that seem to count the most for these teachers. Young people are not naive in their relations with teachers and, in fact, are quite clear about what they want in relationships with them (Beane & Lipka, 1986). Moreover, they are quite capable of discerning sincerity of teacher behaviors and the attitudes those behaviors suggest. This is what the teachers at that workshop saw in the video. And that is one of the reasons why they were attracted to the idea of curriculum integration.

HIGH PEDAGOGY

Anyone who spends any amount of time in the classrooms I have been describing cannot help but marvel at the work of these teachers, especially when there are so many classrooms that seem so dreary and lifeless. Yet these teachers are real people just like their colleagues. They went to schools and colleges and through teacher education programs. They are in relationships with other adults, some have children, and all that I know have interests outside the school and classroom. Moreover, in other classrooms, sometimes even next door, there are very good teachers who use important methods like cooperative learning, unit teaching, portfolios, and the like. But there is something different about *these* classrooms, something that seems almost larger than life. One cannot help but wonder what it is that these teachers believe that turns their classrooms into places of high pedagogy. From listening to their comments and watching them in their classrooms, I think I have an idea.

For one thing, these teachers respect the dignity of young people. They take their ideas, hopes, aspirations, and lives seriously. They listen carefully to young people, whether the message is clear or confused. When asked why they teach this way, these teachers often speak of injustices they have seen done to young people in other classrooms, sometimes in the classrooms of their own schooldays. They accept young people for who they are and do not wish that they had a different group of students in their classrooms.

These teachers believe in democracy and see no reason why democratic values and rights should not be extended to young people in schools. They are interested in and concerned about social issues, enough so that such issues often come to organize work in the classroom. They believe that young people have a right to be well informed and to inquire critically into issues that concern them. They believe that young people have not only a right to have a say in what happens in school, but an obligation to do so. They believe, as my colleague Ed Mikel once said, in "turning the floor over to the traditionally disempowered."

These teachers sincerely believe that diversity in a classroom is a source of strength and possibility rather than a problem. So, for example, they are just as enthused about work from a student who is struggling as from one who is very skilled. They are interested in cultural differences among young people, in high and popular culture, and in so-called youth culture, and they constantly seek ways to bring these out in discussions. And the very design of their work indicates their commitment to making space for various learning styles, modes of expression, and so on.

These teachers want young people to be involved in significant learning around big issues and ideas. Thus the organizing centers for the curriculum involve issues such as conflict, the environment, the future, prejudice and poverty, and the like. Conversely, they have little time for a curriculum that amounts to collecting more and more trivial information or for one that uses themes such as teddy bears, dinosaurs, and apples. Moreover, these teachers are able to keep the focus of work on the big issues while carrying out the day-to-day activities that are smaller parts of those issues.

These teachers have a deep interest in both excellence and equity. They want all young people to do well, to know more, and to be more skilled, including in those areas that are necessary to get through the maze of standardized tests that these teachers almost always despise for their high-culture bias and triviality. This desire for achievement is backed up by a belief that all young people can learn, though not always the same things or at the same level. But the belief that young people can learn and the desire for them to do so lead these teachers to press all young people to do their work well and completely. They do not give up or give in with young people. Yet unlike so many adults, these teachers seem to know what to reasonably expect from young people and how to appreciate what they *can* do rather than harping on what they cannot do.

These teachers seem to believe that life inside and outside the schools should be integrated. As we have already seen, they make room for social

issues, popular culture, and other aspects of life that have often been left
out of the curriculum, as if they did not exist or were not important. But
more than this, these teachers believe young people should have an opportunity to use the resources of the school to deepen their understanding of themselves and their world in terms of their present lives. The curriculum is not simply a farm system for the next grade, or for the next
school level, or for college or work, or for "later in life." And they are genu-
inely interested in those present lives, more so than in external mandates
for content coverage or the rigid scopes and sequences of curriculum
guides.

In describing "these" teachers and their apparent beliefs, I do not mean
to imply that other teachers do not believe many of the same things. Some
certainly do. But the teachers I am speaking of seem, more than others, to
integrate all these beliefs into a coherent pedagogy and to find fulfillment
in helping young people pursue *their* interests and ambitions. And they
seem to live more fully in the world, to be interested in a wide array of
things, especially new ideas they can bring to young people and new ideas
young people bring to them. Again, though, they are not superwomen or
supermen. They are real teachers leading real lives and working in real
schools with real young people.

I am not quite sure how these teachers come to their beliefs. Some
years ago I did a small research study on this question. The teachers involved in that study told me that although teacher education had some
influence on them, their pedagogy followed as much from other sources,
such as time in the Peace Corps, their experiences as students, or their life
philosophies. This actually makes some sense for the work I have described
in this chapter, since it has more to do with a way of thinking than with
instructional techniques. In fact, this pedagogy is a way of life.

Anyone who has ever tried curriculum integration knows that it involves considerable risks both inside and outside the classroom. Stories
abound about the difficult politics of curriculum integration faced by the
teachers I have described in this chapter. But if there is any phrase I consistently hear from them, it is this: "I will never go back." I know of cases
where a few of the teachers have been forced to curtail their work on
curriculum integration to the point where it lost its meaning. Mostly they
moved to other schools that were more conducive to their pedagogy. In
two cases, the teachers actually left the profession. When these teachers
say they will not go back, they mean it. Who can blame them? Why would
they want to leave the place of high pedagogy?

CHAPTER 5

In the Place of Tough Politics

The classrooms we visited in the last chapter are most often exciting and engaging places. But that does not mean that the teachers' work is easy or glamorous. In fact, it is hard work, both intellectually and physically, and more than a little contentious. Anyone who implies otherwise is not telling the truth or not really working on curriculum integration as it is meant to be—or both. Curriculum integration is not for the professionally faint-hearted. Yet too often this approach, like so many other serious curriculum or teaching reforms, is talked about as if it is an easy trick. Nothing could be further from the truth.

INSIDE THE CLASSROOM

Just because life inside classrooms where curriculum integration is used can be interesting and exciting does not necessarily mean that it is easy or always enjoyable. Teachers who use this approach, even those with a good deal of experience, face considerable pedagogical and personal challenges no matter how enthusiastic and committed they are.

Let's face it: Schools are not set up to do curriculum integration. For one thing, resources like textbooks are almost always organized around separate subject or skill areas and are selected by subject-based textbook committees that are unlikely to look beyond their assigned area. Because of this, teachers who use curriculum integration must spend unusual amounts of time finding resources to support their theme-based curriculum. Not surprisingly, such resources can usually be found, since most resources outside the schools are organized around issues rather than subjects, and, once found, these resources are available for future use. Moreover, many textbooks can be useful for some kinds of information. Nevertheless, handing each student a textbook at the beginning of the year and plowing through it is a lot easier than constantly searching for pertinent resources.

Resource availability is not the only thing that makes curriculum integration a challenge for teachers. Nearly all of the school's organizational infrastructure is set up to support a traditional subject-centered, top-down curriculum. Time is allocated (or expected to be allocated) on the basis of separate subject and skill areas. Report cards call for judgments about students' work by subject and skill area. Notebooks, assignment books, and even bookbags are advertised as having separate subject- or skill-area compartments. No matter how comfortable teachers may be with the integration of knowledge, hardly a day goes by without a reminder that other people do not see things the same way. And those other people usually have a lot of tradition on their side.

Then there is the matter of living in a paradigm warp where teachers in search of a better way are also expected to honor the old way. No matter how successful curriculum integration is at promoting a wide range of knowledges, those who use that design typically have to expend a disproportionate amount of time showing how the content and skill from various traditional subjects is still learned—something that colleagues who stick with the old way rarely have to do, no matter the results, since the assumption that mere "coverage equals learning" still holds sway in most professional and public circles. And just as curriculum integration begins to take clear shape for teachers, they are asked to serve on curriculum revision or textbook selection committees organized by separate subject areas.

Furthermore, while teachers who use curriculum integration tend to have better relationships with students than do many of their colleagues, those relationships are still filled with many tensions. As noted in the last chapter, collaborating with students in decision making raises many questions that are ignored in other classrooms: Which students are speaking up and which ones are silent? How do gender, class, and race relations enter into those interactions? Does silence mean consent? Does consent mean commitment? Beyond these questions is the realization that while we can change the curriculum, we cannot so easily change the conditions under which young people live or the experiences they bring with them. In this sense, even something as engaging as curriculum integration done well will not necessarily appeal to all young people. Some who have always been at the top of their class are often uncomfortable with the fact that more of their peers seem to succeed in this approach. Some who have a low tolerance for ambiguity long for the concrete certainty of worksheets and textbooks. Others who have friends in traditional subject-centered programs wonder if required content is being covered. And those whose present lives are overwhelmed with problems or whose previous school experiences have been entirely negative may simply be unable to respond to any curriculum approach.

I am not saying that no other teachers care about such tensions or the problems young people face, but those who have made an explicit commitment to focus the curriculum on self and social meaning must face those issues squarely and with no other "curriculum" to hide behind. This is why, for example, they so often find their classrooms filled with a disproportionate number of students whom other teachers in the building cannot or will not work with. Ironically, such students often appear at the door with a note from the office saying something like this: "He (or she) needs structure." In other words, those responsible for dealing with office referrals and student placements may come to love curriculum integration without knowing or understanding anything about it. All they know is that there seem to be fewer referrals out of those rooms. Meanwhile, for teachers already doing the extra work involved in curriculum integration, the presence of a disproportionate number of these young people can lead to a continuing intensity that threatens to exhaust their energy.

On top of all this, teachers who engage in curriculum integration face the prospect of having to live with constant ambiguity. Granted, many people, including teachers, enjoy some level of ambiguity. But the matter of continuous planning and long-range uncertainty can become wearing when attached to all the other uncertainties of day-to-day life in classrooms. Moreover, teachers are human beings and their lives are not defined by their profession alone. Issues and responsibilities in their lives outside the classroom may at times involve enough ambiguity to strain even the best teacher's tolerance for ambiguity inside the classroom.

AMONG COLLEAGUES

There are very few schools where curriculum integration, as I have defined it, is practiced on a wide scale. Typically the approach is used by a few teachers who have chosen to work this way for reasons quite apart from some schoolwide initiative. Sometimes these teachers are subsequently joined by colleagues who like what they see and want to try something like it themselves. More often, their colleagues seem to shy away from this approach. And almost always, a few engage in serious criticism of curriculum integration and the teachers who use it.

Some of those who shy away from curriculum integration are very good separate-subject teachers. Over time they may have come to love one or more subjects to the point that the subject is a large part of the way they define themselves: "I am a *science* teacher" or "I love teaching *writing*." Others may be less attached to their certification than to beloved activities they have developed over the years: "Each year I can't wait to do butterfly collecting" or "I love my Civil War unit." Again, these may be very fine subject teachers, but they simply cannot imagine the possibility that their beloved subject or activity might somehow get compromised in curriculum integration. Asking them to try out curriculum integration amounts to asking them to reconstruct their professional self-concept. They are convinced that every young person should share their interest and probably would if only given a healthy dose of it.

Moreover, subject-based professional identities are usually tied to status among subject areas—"Math is more important than physical education" and so on—which, in turn, is often tied to who gets preferred schedule slots or who gets which classrooms. Talk about non-subject-area approaches to the curriculum may threaten not only the identities of teachers but the privileges some enjoy as well. Anyone who has ever worked in a school knows that this is very dangerous territory to invade.

Some teachers are reluctant to get involved in curriculum integration projects because they are unsure of how to proceed. That teachers would be unfamiliar with what curriculum integration looks like or how it is done is not surprising given the dominance of the traditional separate-subject, teacher-centered curriculum in schools and teacher education programs. While there are teachers willing to push ahead without a roadmap, many more desire help and support through workshops, study groups, visits to other schools, or partnerships with teachers who have done curriculum integration. Where such opportunities are not available, teachers simply cannot be expected to dive in. In the current climate of antiteacher sentiment, such risks are more than a little dangerous.

However, other colleagues take a dim view of curriculum integration for quite different reasons, though these may not always be completely apparent. They may object on grounds similar to the subject loyalists we just visited or complain that students who came out of curriculum integration arrangements are not sufficiently skilled. They may also claim that they would give it a try except for problems with the schedule or with the report cards or with the resources or with their room assignment or whatever. But behind these objections there is often a deep fear that they might be expected to actually do some integration work in their own classroom. It would be one thing if this reluctance were really about those surface claims. However, it usually has much more to do with a reluctance to get involved with the hard work of this kind of teaching and the sharing of power associated with collaborative planning. After all, one of the best ways to assert control over students is to keep them guessing about what they are supposed to be learning or what might happen next.

At faculty meetings and inside the faculty room and cafeteria, these criticisms take a severe toll on teachers already fatigued by the everyday work of curriculum integration. Moreover, there is nowhere to hide from these kinds of criticisms, since teachers must sooner or later come out of their classrooms. And when they do, curriculum integration itself makes them more vulnerable than they would be if they used a separate-subject approach. Teachers who use a separate-subject approach can hide behind the symbolic walls that surround each subject and claim immunity from pedagogical discussions on the basis of each subject's "uniqueness." As they integrate knowledge, those teachers who use curriculum integration question the "unique" status of individual subjects and thus cannot claim such immunity. As Bernstein (1975) has pointed out:

> Whereas the teaching process under collection [separate-subject approaches] is likely to be invisible to other teachers, unless special conditions prevail, it is likely that the teaching process regulated through integrated codes may well become visible as a result of development in the pedagogy in the direction of flexibility in the structure of teaching groups. (p. 107)

As we shall shortly see, this visibility also makes the teachers vulnerable to criticisms from educational bureaucrats, ambitious parents, and policy pundits. Jousting with these groups is certainly a discouraging experience. However, nothing is more debilitating than knowing that outside the classroom doors, everyday, some colleagues are waiting in ambush. I can recall a time years ago when teachers who used curriculum integration were openly critical of separate-subject loyalists among their colleagues. The teachers I know who do this work today do not seem to be looking for such trouble. They are too busy in their own classrooms. Yet they still seem to suffer severe criticism from some colleagues. Apparently such criticisms do not need to be directly provoked these days. The mere presence of curriculum integration will do.

IN THE GAZE OF AUTHORITY

Those who advocate for the idea of curriculum integration soon discover that the persistence of the traditional subject-centered curriculum is no local accident. Educators inside schools are not the only ones who have trouble with the idea of curriculum integration. No matter how persuasive argument and evidence may otherwise be, subject-centered approaches are protected by the interests of a powerful network of educational elites whose symbiotic relationships are based on the dominance of subjects in curriculum organization.

Among the groups this network includes are many academicians who believe that the one best definition of a "good life" is the intellectual life that they themselves live. While some among these are classical humanists in the great tradition (e.g., Adler, 1982; Bloom, 1987; Hirsch, 1987), others are simply ardent defenders of one or more disciplines of knowledge as the beginning and end of education. Whichever the case, they represent the kind of thinking involved in the Committees of Ten and Fifteen (National Education Association, 1893, 1895) that brought us the subject-centered curriculum at the high school and elementary levels more than a hundred years ago. While other parties in the network have their own areas of authority, these academicians largely define and endorse what Apple (1993) calls "official knowledge." For these academicians, curriculum integration is near the very height of anti-intellectualism and a threat to their very way of life. Some people think about what ought to be the curriculum by looking out at young people and the world. The academicians I am speaking of here think about what ought to be the curriculum by looking in the mirror.

The network also includes college and university teacher educators, most of whom previously taught in schools just like the ones we have now. Not surprisingly, most of them used subject- and skill-centered approaches just like the ones they are hired to teach to prospective teachers. The methods courses they teach are almost always arranged by separate subject and skill areas as mandated by their own interests and by many state accrediting agencies. Requirements aside, it is unrealistic to expect teacher educators who have never used curriculum integration to give much more than lip service to that approach, let alone to suffer the criticisms of colleagues for whom the pedagogical clock stopped the day they left the schools.

A third party to the "network" is the collection of state- and district-level subject supervisors who recommend and audit particular subject matter and skills to be covered by teachers. Though many in this group claim to support curriculum integration, their support usually evaporates right around the boundary of their subject area. This is not surprising, since their job titles are named by separate subjects. One need only walk down the halls of state and district curriculum divisions and read the titles on the doors. Like teachers who are subject loyalists, these bureaucrats usually sense that their area will be compromised by the idea of integration. In some ways, who can blame them? If your job title is a subject name, integration might well seem like an occupational hazard. And in that case, the scopes and sequences of subject areas would surely seem more compelling than the rhythms and patterns of inquiring young minds.

A fourth group in this network includes test and textbook publishers. Here the case is quite simple. These industries take in billions of dollars every year for manufacturing and distributing material based almost entirely on a separate-subject curriculum. A few textbook companies have begun efforts to produce topical and issue-centered resources that will support the work of curriculum integration, and some test makers have tried to push in the direction of applied and context-based assessments. But on the whole, it is laughable to imagine these companies forgoing their profits to advocate for something like curriculum integration, especially without some guarantees of support from other parties in the network.

While it is hard to exaggerate the power of this network of educational "elites," I do not want to imply that it is completely monolithic. Other, equally powerful forces also have interests that can lead to certain kinds of compromises. For example, when business and industry, in league with government agencies, call for skills and predispositions beyond those usually encouraged by a subject-centered curriculum (SCANS, 1992), parties in the network may throw some support behind multidisciplinary approaches that appear to promote complex learning while leaving subject identities intact. Such flexibility is necessary for subject-centered interests to avoid crises in their legitimacy, just as advocates of curriculum integration must often show how subject interests are not altogether ignored in their approach.

In the present politics of curriculum, however, the lines between integration and subject-centered advocacy are reinforced by misdirected criticism of curriculum integration. As suggested in Chapter 3, such criticisms frequently take the form of traditional claims regarding the integrity of the disciplines and their alleged necessity as building blocks for problem solving beyond the disciplines (e.g., Gardner & Boix-Mansilla, 1994). But they also involve questions about the rigor of thematic units (Brophy & Alleman, 1991) and the fate of subject matter in such units (Roth, 1994). Though these sources claim to be criticizing "integration," the examples they use are almost always of the multidisciplinary variety. That the criticisms are, in this sense, ahistorical and theoretically inaccurate is not surprising in the often flimsy world of curriculum debate these days. But for those who are trying to work with curriculum integration in schools, these sloppy criticisms are very painful. Their efforts are called into question, though it is not really their work that is implicated. Nevertheless, these criticisms play well in the current conservative climate where half-truths are as good as gold.

I also want to be clear that when speaking of the network of educational "elites," I am referring to the interests of groups. Not all individuals within one or another of the parties to the network necessarily support its loyalty to subject-centered curriculum and related structures. For example, some disciplinary scholars might well support a high degree of curriculum integration in K–12 schools, regarding serious subject-centered study to be appropriate when students reach colleges and universities. In general, though, the positions of the groups just reviewed are supported by individuals within them. After all, their self-interests are at stake here. The struggles to form, institutionalize, and defend the subject areas have not been easy ones, and neither the subject areas nor the job titles that go with them are going to be given up easily no matter how persuasive the educational arguments to do so (Goodson, 1985; Kliebard, 1986; Popkewitz, 1987).

NOT MY CHILD

Parents and other members of the larger community have been to school themselves, and they know what it usually looks like and how it works. They also have ambitions for children, especially their own. The combination of ambitions and experience helps form expectations of what should happen in the schools. Departures from those expectations tend to make some people nervous. The idea of curriculum integration is no exception to this rule. At the same time, however, understanding how parents and other community members react to curriculum integration is more than a little tricky, since reactions may vary depending on what is expected. Paying attention to these variations can make all the difference in local curriculum politics (Apple, 1996).

There are many parents who are tremendously supportive of the concept of curriculum integration and, in fact, seek to have their children placed in programs where it is used, not only because they are engaging and challenging but because of the democratic values they bring to life. Moreover, some parents welcome such programs simply because they seem to be more engaging than traditional subject-centered arrangements. After all, it is not true that all parents and other adults had wonderful school experiences or found the subject-centered curriculum to be thoroughly engaging or challenging. And we must not forget that in some places programs based on the idea of curriculum integration are in place with the explicit approval of the community, including school boards.

But as with most efforts at curriculum reform, we hear much more about criticisms than about persistent support. For example, some parents are also members of the parties to the network of educational elites I have just described. Not surprisingly, they may object to curriculum integration as parents on the same grounds they object to it professionally. Some parents may simply be caught off guard by the introduction of a new curriculum approach. With other parents, however, the agenda is not always so easily apparent.

Anyone who has seriously advocated for curriculum integration knows the tedium of being asked a thousand times, "But how will students do on standardized tests?" Advocates usually answer that question by reviewing some of the major studies that show that students do at least as well or better and that many teachers report that the approach seems particularly helpful to young people who have traditionally had trouble in school. That response, which does not seem too difficult to understand, nonetheless usually leads to further questioning. Certainly some who raise this question mean it literally. But for others, questions about achievement have a quite different motive.

For many reasons—contextual learning, nonfragmentation, flexible uses of knowledge, and so on—curriculum integration seems to offer greater access to knowledge for more young people. Moreover, because curriculum integration encourages multiple routes to knowledge and multiple ways of demonstrating it, young people who have traditionally monopolized "success" in the classroom are likely to find themselves joined in success by more of their peers. While this may be a surprise to them, it is often profoundly upsetting to some of their parents, whose ambitions for their children include being at the top of the class in school and getting into elite colleges. From these parents, the question about achievement on tests is not a concern about their own children's continued success but about the possibility that their monopoly on success will be threatened (Brantlinger, Majd-Jabbari, & Guskin, 1996).

This concern seems to be particularly prominent in affluent, upper-middle-class areas where parents themselves are faced with growing threats to their professional and management jobs as corporations downsize. Fear for their own privileged positions is easily translated into fear for their children's future economic security (K. S. Newman, 1988; Ehrenreich, 1989). These fears are fed by trumped-up media charges of public school failure and anecdotes of supposedly ill-considered curriculum innovations. In this scenario, something like curriculum integration seems like one more threat to security. That corporate downsizing and diminishing economic security have to do with greed and profits rather than personal competence or school programs does not seem to matter. Apparently neither does the fate of those young people who would continue to be denied access to success in school by a curriculum that is implicated in the disgraceful "sort-and-select" tradition of schools.

Other parents and community members are not so subtle about their objections. It is no secret that we are living in a very conservative era in which historically dominant political and economic groups are noisily reclaiming grounds and goods they believe have been taken away from them by progressives (Apple, 1993). Most of the social roadsigns advise, "Merge right." In the midst of this conservative restoration comes a call for "curriculum integration," an approach, as I have defined it, that is partly rooted in the progressive philosophy of social reconstruction. Unlike many educators who think that curriculum integration is simply about rearranging lesson plans, conservative critics have figured out that it involves something much larger, and they don't like it. For example, here is what the conservative Christian political group, Citizens for Excellence in Education (1992), had to say in their book, *Reinventing America's Schools*:

> Thematic-based curriculum can be used to further a "politically correct" set of values, as James Beane makes clear in his book, *A Middle School Curriculum: From Rhetoric to Reality*. He "argues for a thematic-based curriculum . . . that builds on the interests and concerns of students and society, and addresses student needs for personal, social, and technical skills, while building on a value base that includes democracy, dignity, and diversity." That just about sums up how content focused on values (which many parents object to because it is often infused with secular values that contradict their religious beliefs), so-called "self-esteem," and tolerance can replace academics, when such a teaching method can really be used for either. (p. 48)

In looking at the history of integration in the curriculum, I pointed out that interest in the idea during a period of conservative restoration seems to be a serious contradiction. However, I also argued that this is probably accounted for by the fact that many of the "proponents" of curriculum integration mistakenly limit its definition to a method of correlating subject areas. Now I want to reiterate that claim, using the above quote from one of the most powerful conservative groups in the country as evidence. The point is this: Even the most conservative critics see some benefit in curriculum integration when it is defined simply as a method of rearranging lesson plans. But when its fuller meaning in relation to democratic social integration is used, it is immediately called into question, not only by the ultraconservative critics just named but also by business leaders and privileged parents who otherwise might support the idea. In other words, tinkering with the existing curriculum is not only easier than substantive reform, it is also safer.

Yet another kind of critique emerges from an analysis of curriculum reform based on cultural differences. In this case, curriculum integration and other "progressive" approaches are correctly identified as part of a long line of largely (but not entirely) white, upper-middle-class educational innovations that have often worked from a tacit assumption that the skills upon which school success depends are reinforced by the culture in which the children live. True, the kind of progressive pedagogy I am describing was also proposed by African American educators for schools attended by African American children (Daniel, 1932, 1940; Bond, 1935; Wesley, 1941). But given whose knowledge is taught and tested in most schools and on standardized tests, the assumption of cultural reinforcement was certainly a reasonably safe one for the white upper-middle class. However, it is argued, the same assumption cannot be made for children whose cultures are not of that type, namely, those children who are of different racial, ethnic, and economic backgrounds (e.g., Delpit, 1995). It is these children who have historically been treated most harshly by the "sort-and-select" mechanisms of the schools. And now, just as their scores on standardized tests seem to be rising, progressive educators introduce approaches such as curriculum integration in which test-based skills are neither as visible as they are in the typical subject-centered curriculum nor as relentlessly emphasized.

For this reason, approaches such as curriculum integration seem to move the target of school success and to ignore the fact that children from nonprivileged homes simply may not bring to school with them the cultural codes and skills that are involved in that success. This concern, especially as it is understood by teachers who themselves come from nonprivileged backgrounds, goes a long way toward explaining why approaches such as curriculum integration are often resisted in large urban school districts by educators and noneducators alike. And this concern is likely intensified by the probability that educators from nonprivileged backgrounds may never have seen anything like curriculum integration in their own schooling.

Teachers such as the ones we met in the last chapter do as much as possible to respond to the concerns of parents and other members of the community at large (Brodhagen, 1994, 1995). For example, they often take pains to show the disciplinary sources of much of the knowledge they use, they keep careful records of skills that are taught and how students are doing with them, they invite parents to demonstrations and exhibits of student work, and they use curriculum organizing centers that are substantive, not trivial. They also try to keep the focus of conversations on what young people are learning rather than trying to explain the theory of curriculum integration. In this way, they find common ground with parents and other adults, especially those who are concerned about the skill achievement of nonprivileged young people in the context of curriculum integration.

With some critics, however, there is unfortunately no stable common ground to find in trying to work through objections to curriculum integration. For those who do not really want success for more children and especially for those who want to censor critical inquiry and democratic values, no resolution will satisfy except to abandon the use of curriculum integration. In this case, curriculum integration as I have described it becomes a matter of philosophical debate over the kind of general education that is called for in a supposedly democratic society, a matter that I will take up in Chapter 6. At that level, the debate over curriculum integration is finally seen as part of the long and continuing struggle over the school curriculum (Kliebard, 1986).

MISREADING CURRICULUM INTEGRATION

All of this misperception, apprehension, and critique are complicated by media messages of two types. One is the media's love affair with academic and political conservatives who claim that our civilization (such as it is) is crumbling for the schools' lack of a sufficient dose of high-culture curriculum. People who make their living off words are bound to love lists of words, such as those E. D. Hirsch (1987) and others claim we are all supposed to know. The other type of message is the one that takes the separate-subject curriculum for granted because, after all, media pundits went to the same schools as everyone else and can hardly be expected to imagine something like curriculum integration. This, in turn, feeds the fears of parents who are frightened by anything that varies from the way the world lines up in the mainstream media.

Meanwhile, those school officials who typically communicate with the media have likely had little direct experience with curriculum integration and often misrepresent it to the media with the usual misperceptions that so many educators seem to have. Perhaps the most frequent of these is that curriculum integration, especially as planned with young people, is based on student "interests" or that it is "student-driven." Correctly understood, curriculum integration is driven by the purposes of deepening understanding of self and the world, using knowledge to resolve issues, opening up the curriculum to democractic social integration, respecting the dignity of young people, and building from their diversity. These purposes require applying knowledge, thinking critically, problem solving, and other sophisticated knowledge. This is what makes curriculum integration more challenging, more rigorous, and, to turn a phrase, more "academic" than the separate-subject curriculum. Defining curriculum integration as interest-centered and student-driven inaccurately suggests that it is whimsical and lacking in "rigor." Add the fact that popular culture has a place in this kind of curriculum and the accusations elevate to "anti-intellectual."

I understand that such accusations usually come from people who oppose any kind of progressive work and those who, lacking information

or personal experience, confuse curriculum integration with multidisciplinary units on dinosaurs, teddy bears, the 1960s, and other so-called
appealing topics. But these characterizations are ridiculous. Curriculum
integration is based on concerns of young people and social issues, both of
which may be interesting, but they are not the same as the whimsical
meaning of "interest."

As for rigor, the matter of instrumentally using knowledge to address
self and social issues, which presumes "knowing" content and skill, involves
a very sophisticated kind of intellectualism, as does thoughtful integration of popular- and high-culture knowledge. Questions about rigor ought
to be asked of the separate-subject approach, with its emphasis on accumulation without meaning or application. In this sense, I am continually
amazed by those who would pour money into subject-area commissions
that define challenging content and higher standards by digging deeper
and deeper into academic trivia. The only challenge there is to memory
capacity.

Worse than all that is how some people seem to add up all of the mis-
conceptions about curriculum integration to make it mean nothing more
than a fun time for school malcontents. One national professional news-
letter claimed that my ideas about planning with students were meant to
reduce apathy and rebellion. Imagine that! I was under the impression
that we plan with students because we live in a democracy and it is one of
our obligations to bring the democratic way of life to young people. Actually that writer isn't the only person to make this mistake; perhaps that
says something about how successful the separate-subject curriculum has
been in the area of civic education.

Finally, this tour of some of the politics of curriculum integration would
be incomplete without mention of perhaps the oddest criticism. In reac-
tion to the alleged decline in academic achievement among U.S. students
over the past two decades, some conservative critics have gleefully blamed
"progressive" pedagogy, including curriculum integration. Such an accusation is preposterous since, as we saw earlier, curriculum integration was
almost nowhere to be seen during that period. Thus, if there really has
been a decline in academic achievement (which is not at all clear), approaches such as curriculum integration can hardly be at fault. If anything,
the pedagogy of choice during the period in question was a string of mostly
antiprogressive approaches: "back to the basics," competency-based education, programmed direct instruction, phonics drill, and so on.

Given all of this, it is hardly surprising that advocates of curriculum
integration grow weary of constantly having to defend their work. Nevertheless, as we saw in the last chapter, they push ahead. Granted, though,
it would be a little less exasperating if the questions that are raised about

curriculum integration were also raised about those approaches that are closest to the traditional separate-subject curriculum. Might this happen? Frankly, I doubt it, for reasons that have everything to do with political power and almost nothing to do with the issues at hand. For that reason, regardless of what happens in the classroom, curriculum integration will never be an easy trick. And, for the time being, it is certainly not for the professionally faint-hearted—not when the road to high pedagogy is paved with tough politics.

CHAPTER 6

I Found a National Curriculum

By the year 2000, all students will leave grades 4, 8, and 12 having demonstrated competency over challenging subject matter including English, mathematics, science, foreign languages, civics and government, economics, arts, history, and geography, and every school in America will ensure that all students learn to use their minds well, so that they may be prepared for responsible citizenship, further learning, and productive employment in our Nation's modern economy.

—Goal 3: Student Achievement and Citizenship, Goals 2000: Educate America Act as adopted by Congress, March, 1994

I found a national curriculum. Unlike other people, however, I was not actually looking for one at the time. And, more important, the one I found wasn't where everyone else was looking. I was opposed to having a national curriculum until I found this particular one. Now a national curriculum seems like it might be a good idea, if it is the right kind.

In 1990, I started working with a group of middle school teachers and students on the integrative curriculum design described earlier in Chapter 4. In proposing the design, I had called for the curriculum to be collaboratively planned by teachers and students at the local level so that the questions and concerns raised might be "real" to those involved in any place where the curriculum was undertaken. In starting the first group, I designed a rather obvious process for collaborative planning within the design. I say "obvious" because the first step in the collaborative planning simply replicated the theory by asking the students to identify questions they had about themselves and their world and then asking them to talk with one another to find those they shared in common.

Our first theme, "Living in the Future," included personal questions, such as "How long will I live?" and "What will I look like when I am older," and world questions about the environment, technology, war, and so on in the future. To address these questions, we worked with the students to design activities, such as having an artist sketch them as they might look later in life, finding predictions made for our own time to see if they had actually happened, conducting a survey of students in other schools to see what they thought might happen in the future, and making recommendations for what our city should be like in the year 2020.

In short, the unit was a real success, enough so that the teachers decided to continue using the curriculum design the next year with a new group of students. That experience was also successful, and we began to tell the story of our work (Brodhagen et al., 1992). In addition, the teachers were filmed doing the planning with students and featured on a national video teleconference.

As a result of all this, we were asked to conduct workshops about the curriculum, including demonstrations of how we planned with students. Since 1992, we have conducted simulations of our planning process with thousands of adults from virtually every state. We have also demonstrated the planning with thousands of students in schools around the country and heard from many teachers who have done the same planning on their own. And on several occasions we have planned with mixed groups of young people and adults. Doing these planning sessions is how I found a national curriculum.

We have planned in cities, suburbs, and rural towns. Participants have been of widely diverse backgrounds in terms of race, class, gender, geography, age, and so on. Always we ask the same two questions: What questions do you have about yourself? What questions do you have about your world? No matter where we go, the same responses seem to emerge over and over. How long will I live? Will there be enough money in the future? Will I be successful? Do other people think I am the way I think I am? Will my family stay together? Will there be world peace? Why do people hate each other? When will violence stop? Will cures be found for cancer and AIDS? Will the environment survive? What will technology bring us? Will there ever be a president who is not a white man? Will hunger end? Why are there so many poor people? Moreover, as participants cluster their questions, the same themes come up time and time again: The Future, Conflict and Violence, The Environment, Health and Disease, Government and Politics, and so on.

Here, then, is the substance of a national curriculum. People all around the United States, people of various ethnicities, races, socioeconomic levels, geographic areas, genders, ages, and occupations seem to have basically the same questions and to be concerned about the same general issues. These questions and issues are, in that sense, one of the things we share in common as people of a nation (even though some people may not have these questions or know that others do). They are for us and they are about us. They are what we worry about and what we want to know.

They are, more than any of the lists of facts and skills that someone says everyone should know, a national curriculum. While commissions and associations search for that elusive "common ground," struggling over contentious politics regarding one set of facts or another, I have actually met a national curriculum. Not surprisingly, it is about us.

My claim may seem wild and irresponsible to the lovers of fact and skill lists and the privileged who mistrust the cultures and motives of everyone but themselves and their friends. After all, we live in an era of conservative restoration carried out through the heavy-handed politics of authoritarian populism (Apple, 1993, 1996). A curriculum organized around significant societal issues and with room for classroom-level planning has neither the content nor process controls of the discipline-centered, top-down juggernaut called the "national standards movement." But I don't think my claim is wild at all. The reason is that we supposedly live in a democracy and, if we take that concept seriously, the curriculum I am describing is just the kind we might expect for a national curriculum.

GENERAL EDUCATION, 1990s STYLE

A major reason for maintaining schools is to bring young people into contact with ideas beyond their immediate experience—ideas that connect them with other people, places, and events that are part of the wider human community. This connection is so important that it is among the reasons why attendance in schools (or approved equivalents) has been compulsory in the United States. Where particular ideas or experiences are deemed to be of crucial importance, they are expected to be included in the planned curriculum for all young people or in what is called "general education." This does not mean that all young people would take away precisely the same meanings from such a curriculum but rather that it would constitute a common set of events in which they would participate. At its simplest level, this line of reasoning is the foundation for a national curriculum: All young people ought to share a common curriculum—a general education—that connects them to others at a national level in a shared experience with ideas that are deemed to be of great importance.

That reasoning goes along very nicely, of course, until it comes to the inevitable double-edged question: Which ideas are of such importance that all people should have contact with them *and* who says so? Needless to say, this question makes the concept of a general education, and especially a national curriculum, very slippery territory. Yet a surprising number of people and groups seem more than willing, anxious even, to walk boldly into that territory. In fact, proposals for a national curriculum have become something of an educational industry.

The most obvious example of this rush to mandate is the many commissions and committees that have feverishly drafted "national standards." A hundred years ago there were the Committee of Ten and the Committee of Fifteen; now there are at least ten or fifteen committees. Taken together, these groups have supposedly figured out what every young person should know in virtually every subject area imaginable as part of initiatives like the Goals 2000: Educate America Act. Of course, to build consensus around any given set of standards has required omission or deletion of anything that might be contentious to particular interest groups, such as those that are the vanguard of the new conservatism. Thus the lists of standards are not only long, but sterilized as well. And although there has been some talk about working across subject areas, the history of curriculum tells us that the version of general education most likely to emerge from this "standards movement" is almost certain to be a late-twentieth-century rehash of the same separate-subject curriculum that has served the broader purposes of schooling so poorly for so long.

Those groups are not the only participants in the current general education debate. Other groups, such as the U.S. Department of Labor (SCANS, 1992), have proposed basing the curriculum on those skills and attitudes that business and industry leaders desire in the labor pool. And individuals such as E. D. Hirsch (1987) have filled bookshelves with their own pronouncements. The history of these ad hoc and individual platforms is as old as whenever someone first thought that everyone should know some particular thing. Besides those of highly visible individuals and groups, these kinds of proposals also include beliefs about general education held by individual teachers and parents. In fact, while the former are more widely known, the latter are likely more powerful in the everyday lives of children.

Until recently, the longstanding debate over general education in the United States consisted largely of point/counterpoint recommendations by various individuals and groups whose arguments were more or less influential in the minds of educators and the general public (e.g., Corey & Others, 1942; Harvard University, 1945; G. H. Henry, 1956; Beane, 1980; Adler, 1982; Hirsch, 1987). This was not necessarily because the citizens of this country liked a good debate, but because, unlike in most other countries, the Constitution of the United States leaves regulation of educational programs to individual states rather than the federal government. Thus the word *national* in relation to standards does not technically mean national *regulation* in the same way as the word *federal* would. But listen to the rhetoric: a compendium of "national" standards (or state standards validated by a national board or state standards so widely shared across states as to constitute a de facto national curriculum), aligned with a system of national tests, as part of a government-sponsored effort to raise academic standards. What else could this be but a national curriculum?

Clearly, then, the long-debated concept of general education has been elevated to a new level. We are not simply talking about a de facto national curriculum defined by textbook companies or standardized test manufacturers. No longer are we talking about one or another group or individuals trying to persuade whoever would listen regarding some version of what young people ought to know or be able to do or value. Instead, we are now arguing over the content of a national curriculum that may not necessarily be regulated by federal law but will surely press hard on schools everywhere as it is buttressed by national testing, national validation of state standards, and the inevitable desire of real estate agents to sell homes in states and communities whose schools have a curriculum that "meets national standards."

Aside from the obvious constitutional matter, there are plenty of arguments for and against a national curriculum (Apple, 1996). On the plus side is the possibility of upgrading the curriculum possibilities for those young people who attend the most underresourced schools (although to be honest, the national will to support equitable schools seems to have altogether vanished). Also, for those who don't like whatever the curriculum is, jousting with the windmill of one national version would be a lot easier than with 50 versions. On the negative side, a national curriculum is bound to present almost only the views of the dominant culture. While this has always been the case anyway, there is probably a better chance of arguing against monoculturalism at the local level where nondominant cultures are not so invisible as they are in national politics. Furthermore, there is the not-so-small matter of whether those who would get to have a say in what constitutes the national curriculum are worthy of the national trust.

But beyond all of this, there is something very troubling about the way the steamroller called "national standards" is bearing down on the schools. In a nutshell, the curriculum that is likely to emerge from the standards movement is not a very good one. There are two reasons. One has to do with who decides about the curriculum. The other has to do with what the curriculum is about.

WHOSE NATIONAL CURRICULUM?

In a democracy, people are supposed to have a say about what affects them. Surely this would include a so-called national curriculum, since by virtue of compulsory education nearly everyone would be affected. And for those few who have no direct, personal link to the schools—they've already graduated, have no children or grandchildren in the neighborhood—there is still a right to participate if we believe that schools actually have some impact on the nation as a whole. Therefore, we should expect that a national curriculum would emerge from some process that involves much more widespread participation than has been the case with the national standards to date. This process would also include young people, since surely they are most directly affected, and I can find nothing in the laws of the land—the Constitution, the Bill of Rights, and so on—that prohibits their having a say in the curriculum.

What if the questions and concerns that people identify as sources of the curriculum are different over time or from place to place? Certainly people are likely to differ to some extent regarding what needs attention. And they are almost sure to change their minds over time. But this is one of the key points about a democratic curriculum that elite committees miss entirely in their isolated deliberations. A curriculum that is planned locally and subject to change is much more responsive to emerging issues than one that is centrally determined and thought to be permanent. What if one or another locale misses some large issue or concern that virtually everyone else has identified? As if that doesn't happen now. But here is where federal oversight might actually be helpful—not in terms of enforcing compliance but in supporting widespread communication about what is happening in various locales with regard to which issues are being used to organize the curriculum, how plans are being made, what resources are being used, what projects are being undertaken, what is being learned from these experiences, and so on.

In suggesting that a truly national curriculum would need a large dose of local planning, I am quite aware of the possibility that local choices and decisions are not always for the common good. After all, were it not for the Constitution and the courts, local officials in many places would still legally segregate schools by race and exclude young people with handicapping conditions. This is why we have federal laws and regulations. But what if the selection of content or issues or materials or ideas is biased by local opinion or prejudice? The fact is, no matter how tightly defined any curriculum plan, it is virtually certain to be mediated by local views.

It is true that the curriculum almost everywhere is shaped by widely held expectations regarding basic skills, by goals and mandates that are remarkably similar across states and local districts, by nationally administered standardized tests, and by widely distributed resources such as textbooks and taped television documentaries. But it is also true that the curriculum is shaped by the local politics of textbook selection, the demands of special-interest groups, the desires of various parents, the aspirations of particular students, and, of course, the beliefs of teachers who finally decide about the curriculum when they close their classroom doors. To imagine, even for a minute, that the politics of curriculum is without local flavor is absurd.

But isn't the point of a national curriculum to be sure that everyone everywhere is taught the same thing in school? Try as they might to deny it, those who have been involved in making long lists of standards in various subjects must have this in mind. Otherwise, why would they call their lists "national" standards and plan to tie them to national tests? Even though, after some resistance from localized groups, states have suddenly been invited to substitute their own standards, the latter are still expected to be reviewed by a national oversight group and enforced through state-sponsored tests.

The point is that the idea of a fully prescribed, detailed national curriculum is unworkable no matter what. For one thing, virtually all top-down educational prescriptions are mediated by local interests. For another, there are real people living in those local communities, and when they come to school, their realities come with them. Most people like their local quirks, and they don't like to be told they shouldn't. This doesn't mean all those quirks are good. As I said before, sometimes they are bad enough to require judicial intervention. But when people believe they live in a democratic society, there is simply no sense in trying to deny them their right to have a say.

On the other hand, if we are to be a society bound together in part by some shared educational experience, then the idea of "national" curriculum is not entirely farfetched. Moreover, such a curriculum idea cannot be dismissed solely on the grounds that it might violate inevitable local customs. But if a "national" curriculum is meant to bring us together, why do the current national standards committees think only in terms of their own compartmentalized academic interests as they construct lists of facts and skills that they think everyone else should know? Such a narrow way of thinking about who should determine a "national" curriculum is hardly becoming in what claims to be a democratic society. Why not imagine a way of creating a national curriculum that is more closely aligned with the idea of democracy? Why not at least begin with one of the major tenets of democracy: faith in the capacity of people to work out intelligent solutions to issues that face them? If there is a need for a national curriculum, why not frame it partly around a process by which there would be widespread and continuous participation in considering what that curriculum ought to be about?

A CURRICULUM ABOUT WHAT?

The work of democracy is the collaborative and intelligent consideration of those issues, problems, and concerns that are shared across the society and its geographical, age, race, class, ethnic, gender, and other diversities. If schools really are supposed to play a crucial role in maintaining and extending the democratic way of life, we should expect, then, that such issues would play a prominent role in the organization and content of the general education curriculum. I have already reported that when we have asked people to identify questions and concerns they have about themselves and the world, they have responded by naming widely shared issues: living in the future, conflict and prejudice, distribution of wealth and justice, environmental problems, mental and physical health, political inequities, and the like. When issues like these become organizing centers for the curriculum, as they are researched and debated, and as their possible resolution is imagined, the school curriculum brings the work of democracy to life. In a democracy, this is exactly what we should expect a national curriculum to do.

A national curriculum should bring young people together to experience democracy and the democratic way of life. This means learning to work together on issues of shared concern. It means learning to integrate self-interest with concern for the common good. It means learning to intelligently apply knowledge to the resolution of substantive issues. It means learning to critically inquire into problematic situations. It means learning about diverse ideas and opinions. It means working on real problems that real people have in their real lives.

This version of a general education curriculum is quite different from the one that is likely to emerge from the national standards movement as envisioned by Ravitch (1995) and other national curriculum "standard-bearers." The standards movement is aimed at mastery of content from various subject areas, not the use of knowledge in relation to real-life issues or the integration of knowledge that is necessary for real-life situations. Nor will the traditional subject of social studies suffice for such a general education curriculum, since it almost always confuses coverage of chronological history with citizenship education. I am not suggesting here that discipline-based knowledge is useless or irrelevant in real-life situations; as I showed in Chapter 3, such knowledge is often exactly what is needed. But the disciplines themselves simply do not make sense as the organizing concept for a general education curriculum.

Unfortunately, the standards-based curriculum is almost certain to be organized around the traditional school subjects since the authors of the standards are drawn mostly from the ranks of subject-area associations and academic disciplinarians. Not surprisingly, all of the standards developed to date are laid out according to separate-subject categories. There has been talk of finding multidisciplinary or interdisciplinary links across the standards, but only the historically naive could seriously believe that this will happen on a large scale where the starting point was mastery of subject matter from within various subject areas. Besides, looking for common ground where subject areas overlap is not at all the same as starting with problems or issues that face people in a democratic society.

By arguing for a general education that is organized around widely shared issues and problems, I am not rejecting the possibility that some portion of a school's program would be organized around separate subjects. However, in elementary and middle school an issue-centered general education should comprise nearly the whole of the curriculum and dominate the school schedule. As young people reach high school, their aspirations may lead toward studies within particular subjects, and although I am not completely sold on this, it may be appropriate to consider ideas in their subject categories, abstracted from the issues of larger life. But at the most, such a "specialized" curriculum should not form more than a portion of the school program, nor should it be mistaken for what ought to be a "general" education curriculum in a democratic society. More precisely, a separate-subject curriculum should be understood for what it is: an abstract organization of content and skill that is meant for pursuance of greater degrees of specialization and differentiation. Such a curriculum may be appropriate for some purposes, but it does not qualify as an appropriate version of a "national" curriculum.

A NATIONAL CURRICULUM WORTH THE NAME

The people of the United States face many very difficult issues: sharp divisiveness among interest groups, huge disparities in the distribution of wealth, erosion of environmental protection, continuing injustice toward minority groups, and more. The fate of the nation largely rests on whether issues such as these can be resolved for the benefit of the common good. Moreover, they will need to be resolved by people, including young people, for they will not simply go away by any other means. Yet as these issues intensify, as the pressure mounts, what do elite academicians, politicians, and media pundits envision for a "national" curriculum for our schools? Larger doses of fragmented information and skills divided into separate subject categories that are remote from compelling issues in the larger world.

If there was a national curriculum, it ought to be about life as it is widely lived by the people of the nation. It ought to address their needs, interests, problems, and concerns as they see them. It ought to contribute to the common good of the society as a whole. It ought to bring diverse young people together in a democratic experience. It ought to be about something of great personal and social significance to young people. Yes, there may be other things that are done in school programs, things that are meant to help meet individual aspirations or interests. But the general education portion, the part that would be "national" in scope, ought to be something other than more of the traditional subject-centered curriculum. It ought to be about bringing democracy itself to life in both the process by which the curriculum is planned and the substance that it involves.

Those who are pushing for a national curriculum in the United States are, unfortunately, driven by motives that are not nearly as elevating as a vision of general education that extends the democratic way of life and takes on the great issues that face us. Instead, they speak of using the schools to improve the skills of students who will be available to business and industry. And they speak of an academic crackdown on young people by requiring them to master more subject-based information, while cleverly protecting the traditional territories in the separate-subject curriculum.

Those groups claim to be looking for a national curriculum. But I suspect their search has more to do with self-interest than the common good. This is why they end up looking in all the wrong places. To find a national curriculum worth having, one needs to inquire into those concerns that are widely shared by the people of a nation rather than the narrow aims of academic or economic self-interest. This is what happened in those workshops where we asked people to identify questions they had about themselves and their world. Wherever we went, across all kinds of diversities, the same issues seemed to come up. I have been very careful here to refer to what I found as *a* national curriculum, not *the* national curriculum. I do not want to seem overly ambitious and, besides, I wasn't looking for a national curriculum. But what I found sure looks like one to me.

CHAPTER 7

How Fares Curriculum Integration?

A few years ago I submitted a paper arguing for curriculum integration to a well-known educational journal. Soon thereafter the editor called to discuss some changes that needed to be made. At the end of the conversation, he said this: "I know you're right about this idea, but it terrifies me. So much would have to change." Thinking now about that statement, I agree with him on every count. Having worked in classrooms where curriculum integration is used, I do believe that it is a powerful and important idea. But I am also terrified because it is so very different from the kind of curriculum that is offered in most schools and so much will need to change if it is to have a more secure place in the educational scene than it does now. As I have said repeatedly, curriculum integration is not simply a method for rearranging lesson plans, as so many educators seem to think. Rather it is a broad theory of curriculum design that encompasses particular views about the purposes of schools, the nature of learning, the organization and uses of knowledge, and the meaning of educational experience.

One mark of its distinctiveness is that where curriculum integration has been used, it has often attracted a variety of critics who find fault with the idea for one reason or another (or many). Paul George (1996) identified no less than 35 reasons why educators should be cautious about curriculum integration. What is it that causes so many people to wring their hands for so many reasons? To answer this question, we must recall the claims that are actually made by advocates of curriculum integration:

- The schools have an obligation to promote democratic social integration through persistent use of democratic practices such as heterogeneous grouping, participatory planning, and collaborative problem solving.
- A general education curriculum for a democratic society ought to be organized around personal and social/world concerns.
- Learning about and working on social/world issues gives young people experience with democratic problem solving.
- Young people have a democratic right to participate in planning the school curriculum and to have their ideas taken seriously.

- Learning to participate in collaborative planning is a critical citizenship skill in a democratic society.
- Making room for personal concerns in the curriculum gives students a stake in the curriculum and encourages the integration of experience.
- Everyday knowledge and experience as well as popular culture ought to be as important in the school curriculum as the disciplines of knowledge.
- Significant self and social/world issues offer a meaningful context for bringing knowledge to young people.
- The primary use of knowledge in the curriculum ought to be in responding to significant self and social issues.
- Understanding and working on significant self and social issues requires (re)integration of knowledge.
- (Re)integrated knowledge most nearly resembles the organization of knowledge as it is used in everyday life outside of educational institutions.

I began this book with a similar summary of the claims made for curriculum integration and rhetorically asked how anyone could object to it. In the end, and beyond the review of political matters in Chapter 5, I think it is important to ask why it is that curriculum integration has never gained the kind of ascendance that other curriculum forms have.

FACING REALITY

I do not believe that advocates of curriculum integration (as I have described it) really expect that it will gain ascendance in every school. That would deny the whole history of the coexistence of conflicting curriculum forms on the school landscape (Kliebard, 1986). But more than that, curriculum integration faces several dilemmas that other forms, such as those tied to classical disciplines or economic interests, do not.

One dilemma is that curriculum integration involves a bottom-up planning structure. As with other educational ideas that embody democracy, curriculum integration involves loosening the grip of centralized authority and emphasizing curriculum planning by teachers and students at the classroom level. At the same time that this frees teachers and students from various obstacles, it also runs counter to the long history of attempts to bureaucratically control what goes on in classrooms. For example, as teachers and students organize knowledge in relation to the issues they are working on, they are less likely to follow detailed scope-and-sequence prescriptions developed in state- and district-level offices. As they make space in the curriculum for popular-culture issues and resources, teachers and students are likely to stray from knowledge that has been given official sanction by academicians, textbook publishers, and others. And in attempting to create democratic communities in their classrooms, they are likely to replace many of the time, space, and communication structures that are pretty well standardized in schools.

The flexibility involved in curriculum integration presents a troubling contradiction for its advocates. While they may desire more widespread use of the approach, the fact that it leans heavily on classroom-level planning means that it cannot be turned into a new set of detailed forms that might replace the bureaucratic structures that support a classical, separate-subject curriculum. One way in which this issue arises is in the question of how coordination and articulation might be assured in the curriculum of a whole school or district if the process of curriculum planning were to begin with collaborative teacher–student planning across all, or even most, classrooms. The same question, of course, applies at any level beyond the classroom.

An obvious way out of this dilemma is to understand curriculum integration as a framework for the curriculum that involves several concepts: organizing centers drawn from significant self and social issues, collaborative planning, integration of knowledge, applied projects, and so on. Thus the idea of flexibility does not mean that teachers and students are free to do whatever they please, but rather that they are able to work out the specific ways of bringing that framework to life. While there may be great diversity across classroom situations, all would be engaged with the same general curriculum. In other words, coordination would be found in the framework for the curriculum rather than the details of its implementation.

Part of such an arrangement would be to finally accept the fact that curriculum, teaching, and learning are very complicated matters and that ways of learning, especially, are often quite personal. Thus it simply makes more sense to spend our time and energy figuring out how to work with that variability than it does to continue trying to invent schemes to force all young people to learn the same things in the same ways and at the same rates. Thinking about a curriculum whose organizing centers emerge from classroom planning, for example, might raise many intriguing questions. What if a group names the same theme two years in a row? Is it merely repetition if the questions within the theme are different, the resources more sophisticated, the projects more demanding, and so on? Might a group make general plans for itself over a two- or three-year period so as to suggest its own pattern of articulation? Could the possibility for coherence and articulation be better assured by having one or two teachers stay with a particular group of students for two or three years?

Imagining ways of simultaneously supporting coordination *and* flexibility would certainly be intriguing. However, it is unlikely that such arrangements would offer the level of increased central control that various interest groups seek to exercise over the curriculum. Nor would they likely allow for the precise alignments that are involved with current mechanisms of control: standardized tests (where billions of dollars of profits are at stake), prescribed scope-and-sequence packages, curriculum maps, territorial lists of required content items, uniform textbook adoptions, and so on. In fact, to allow for such things would necessitate such a severe case of what Powell, Skoog, Troutman, and Jones (1996) have called "theoretical downsizing" that what would be left of "curriculum integration" would hardly fit its definition.

A second dilemma also follows from the bottom-up, "situational" structure of curriculum integration. In this case, the fact that authentic curriculum integration depends partly on collaborative planning with each particular group of students in each classroom or school location means that it cannot be bought or sold as a curriculum package. Put another way, the specific curriculum plans developed collaboratively in any one classroom are meant for people in that situation and are not meant to be prescribed for other classrooms. This is why advocates are often reluctant to answer specific implementation questions. It is not that they lack answers, but giving them would imply that others should do exactly as they do.

The local, collaborative planning involved in curriculum integration suggests the possibility that teachers might reclaim some measure of control from the bureaucratic and management schemes that have increasingly regulated curriculum and teaching. In this sense, curriculum integration involves not only relative autonomy in curriculum planning but also professional knowledge, skill, and inclination to use that autonomy. Ironically, though, many teachers have expressed a desire for specific instructions on all aspects of classroom management as well as prepared curriculum units that might be used.

To deliver on these requests would again be to risk the possibility of "theoretical downsizing" suggested by Powell and his colleagues (1996). Yet one cannot blame these teachers entirely for their desire for explicit direction. As we saw earlier, it is very likely that many, if not most, would have encountered nothing like curriculum integration either in their own schooldays or in their teacher education programs. And, in the intensity of their professional lives—the exhaustion of the teaching day, the lack of planning time, the push to cover more in less time, and so on—there is bound to be a certain appeal in the junk-mail advertisements for commercial curriculum packages and the possibility of simply posting queries for teaching ideas on Internet listserves.

This does not mean that there is nothing at all that teachers might rely on as they begin to work with the idea of curriculum integration. As I indicated in Chapter 2, a growing number of books and articles have appeared in the last few years in which teachers already experienced in the approach have offered detailed accounts of their own work. Many also offer presentations at various professional conferences. Moreover, there are teachers to consult with in virtually every school or district who have used at least some of the ideas involved in curriculum integration, albeit perhaps behind closed classroom doors. And surely the theory of curriculum integration itself must offer some hint of classroom ideas. But beyond this, if what is to be done is what curriculum integration was truly meant to be, there can be no recipes.

Advocates of curriculum integration are already in the difficult position of promoting a complex pedagogy that requires a large measure of autonomy and creativity. That position is only made more difficult by the fact that they must simultaneously compete with the siren song of commercially prepared curriculum packages and the comparatively easy systems offered by proponents of multidisciplinary curriculum models.

A third, and even more serious, dilemma has to do with the values curriculum integration embodies. Criticisms of curriculum integration most often seem to begin with questions about how young people will subsequently fare on standardized tests of academic achievement. Based on the comparative studies with the separate-subject approach noted in earlier chapters, advocates of curriculum integration claim that students in classrooms where the approach is used will not experience a decline in standardized test scores and will not be disadvantaged if and when they encounter subject-centered curriculum arrangements later on in school or college.

As I pointed out earlier, however, the evidence on this matter rarely ends the debate, since fear of failure on standardized tests is not really what is on the minds of many critics. Rather, it is the values that curriculum integration embodies: the emphasis on democratic practices, the concern for wider access to knowledge, the recognition of everyday knowledge and popular culture, the critical analysis of social issues, and so on. In the end, curriculum integration is criticized not for what it doesn't do but for *what it does do*. For if we look across the history of schooling in this country, including many of the so-called reforms that are now being proposed, the record with regard to those values is not a pretty picture and one must sometimes wonder if it was ever meant to be.

We in the United States live within the structures of capitalism, with concepts such as competition and individualism elevated to the status of moral virtues. Reinforcing these concepts is necessary to maintain the appearance that socioeconomic privilege has been "earned" by all those who have it and to explain away the many inequities that so visibly contradict the fundamental concepts of democracy and human dignity. What, then, would lead any of us to believe that a curriculum form meant to promote democratic practice, critical analysis of social issues, collaborative problem solving, and democratic social integration would rest easy in the schools of such a society—especially the schools—where the young are to learn their important social lessons.

Other curriculum forms are more suited to those lessons: the classical subject-area approach that distances knowledge from the everyday lives of the nonprivileged or the programs aimed at preparing young people to fill the labor needs of large corporations. It is hardly surprising that there is a more secure place for these forms than for an approach such as curriculum integration.

I am not unaware that these issues are hard ones for many people to face up to. Some may even think that it is foolish to bring up such problems in a book that is meant to explain a curriculum approach and perhaps to gently encourage more educators to give it a try. Why complicate things when they are beginning to move along a bit? But the bigger mistake would be to pretend that such matters have no relation to the selection and use of various curriculum approaches, and anyone who ventures into curriculum integration as I have described it might as well do so with their eyes wide open. Besides, I want to offer something of a challenge to those very fine professional educators, and others, who are already dabbling with ideas such as curriculum integration because they want school to be a better, more humane place for young people. If we can see our way to changing those aspects of schools that do not "respect children," why do we shy away from also naming conditions in the larger world that do not "respect" them? Is it possible that we might now see that working on an approach such as curriculum integration is not only about helping young people to learn more and making the school a more engaging place? Might we now see that it is also an effort to make good on the school's obligation to extend democracy, respect human dignity, and celebrate diversity?

In facing these political realities, I certainly do not want to leave the impression that the prospects for more widespread use of curriculum integration are hopeless. In fact, there are several signs that interest in the approach is growing. One is the increasing number of books, articles, workshops, and conferences about curriculum arrangements beyond the separate-subject approach, many of them decidedly in the direction of what I have described as curriculum integration. These are, of course, in addition to the many continuing integrative projects and programs that have persisted in various areas, such as early childhood education. In addition, there will surely be further advances out of related efforts around such ideas as democratic schools, the project approach, constructivism, and problem-focused arrangements initiated within subject-area associations linked to social studies, science, family and consumer science, language arts, and more. Some of these cannot go much longer without finally letting go of their subject-area ties and confronting the fuller implications of their work.

This point about seeing hope in related movements is very important. As an advocate for curriculum integration, I have tried to take an uncompromising stand in describing the meaning of the approach, in this book and elsewhere. This is not simply a clever trick, since I really am committed to the position as taken. But as I indicated earlier, curriculum integration does not involve a recipe or packaged program. In the end it is not an "ideal state" to be achieved but rather an idea that is constantly struggled over by those who work with it.

Teachers (and others) who work with curriculum integration are constantly confronted with a variety of questions. How might we plan with students? What knowledge is surfacing in projects, and is it being approached with sufficient depth and breadth? When should the teacher intervene or, alternately, stay out of the deliberations of students? What size chunk of a broad issue or problem should be taken on in a unit? Do the questions associated with a unit address the really crucial aspects of an issue or problem? What knowledge deemed crucial by external agencies, or even by the teacher, is really crucial for young people? Who should have what degree of say in questions about knowledge, assessment, theme identification, and so on?

Since the theory of curriculum integration offers no definitive answers to these questions, there might be many kinds of responses. This means, in turn, that there may be many paths that people can take along the way to exploring curriculum integration. In the end, the issue is not the particular answers to those kinds of questions but the philosophical and pedagogical principles of curriculum integration. As we answer practical questions about implementation of the idea, are we seeking to further the possibility that young people will be able to personally integrate their educational experiences? Do our answers promote democratic social integration, striving for a sense of unity across the diversities in the group? Are we drawing from a variety of sources of knowledge, without regard for subject-area lines, as those are pertinent to the problem or issue at hand? Do our answers sustain a problem-focused, integrative organization of the curriculum?

Understanding this difference between recipe-like answers and answers that seek to pursue guiding principles finally stands, then, as a source of optimism regarding the prospects and possibilities for curriculum integration. If I were to count the number of teachers I know who are doing curriculum integration almost exactly as I have described it, the number would be very small (though growing). On the other hand, if we were to take into account all those teachers who are working at the idea of curriculum integration, some behind closed doors with subject-area labels, the number would be much, much larger. And surely as the current efforts to protect the classical subject-area curriculum fail to deliver an education that is intellectually stimulating, academically challenging, and socially conscious, more and more educators will sense that perhaps there may be something to this idea of curriculum integration after all.

HOW FARES CURRICULUM INTEGRATION?

Those of us who now advocate for curriculum integration stand on the shoulder of giants who have gone before us in this work. We are part of a long line that began decades ago and in which we are the latest participants. As I look around today, I understand as well as anyone the challenge before us. It may be that our present work will be blocked entirely by those who want a rigid, predetermined curriculum that satisfies the adult craving to push their own interests and desires onto children. It may be that our voices will be drowned out by those who want a sterile curriculum that inhibits young people from pursuing their right to an education that engages them with significant self and social issues. It may be that we will be brushed aside by those who want authoritarian control over the minds of young people—those who would protest a curriculum that encourages young people to use their minds to think critically about the world and to construct their own meanings. It may be that we will collapse under the weight of criticism from colleagues who see correctly that this kind of teaching is more complex, more difficult, and more tiring than the use of prepackaged lesson plans.

All of these things are possible; in some places where progressive teachers are especially isolated, these things may even be probable. Even if we do end up as the passing fad that some people think we are, we will not have failed altogether. This is the work that is meant to bring the fundamental concepts of democracy, dignity, and diversity to life in the school curriculum. So it is that no matter what, when educational historians search among the rubble of our times, they will find evidence that there were at least some who tried to keep the work alive.

A headquarters staff person in a national association supposedly once said that I alienate people because I insist on connecting this line of curriculum work with the obligation to take on social problems. That criticism suggests just the kind of failure of nerve that trivializes potentially significant curriculum reform. I do believe that curriculum integration is among those ideas that might help young people to have the predispositions and skills that are needed to solve social problems and improve society, and so do the many others who advocate for and work with the idea. We are not unmindful of how complex the matter of school effects is. But why else would we do this work? Why else would we have a curriculum? Why else would we have schools?

Those of us who advocate for curriculum integration believe that young people have a right to be intelligent, to be well informed, to search for meaning in their world, to be engaged with significant issues, to do authentic work, to learn the whole story, to think critically, to form values, to make judgments, and to be respected. We believe that our work can help young people with those things, and we have seen that it does. This is why you will hear teachers and others who are involved with this approach say they will never go back to the old way. They will never go back. For this reason, more than any, while the gains are still relatively small, the challenges great, and the obstacles large, curriculum integration fares well today, and it will not go away.

Bibliography

Adler, Mortimer. (1982). *The Paideia proposal*. New York: Macmillan.

Aikin, Wilford. (1942). *The story of the Eight Year Study*. New York: Harper & Row.

Alberty, Harold. (1948). *Reorganizing the high school curriculum*. New York: Macmillan.

Alberty, Harold. (1960). Core programs. In *Encyclopedia of educational research* (3rd ed., pp. 337–341). New York: Macmillan.

Alberty, Harold B., & Alberty, Elsie J. (1962). *Reorganizing the high school curriculum* (3rd ed.). New York: Macmillan.

Alexander, Wallace M., with Carr, Dennis, & McAvoy, Kathy. (1995). *Student-oriented curriculum: Asking the right questions*. Columbus, OH: National Middle School Association.

Alpern, Morton (Ed.). (1967). *The subject curriculum: Grades K–12*. Columbus, OH: Merrill.

Apple, Michael W. (1990). *Ideology and curriculum* (2nd ed.). London and Boston: Routledge & Kegan Paul.

Apple, Michael W. (1993). *Official knowledge: Democratic education in a conservative age*. New York and London: Routledge.

Apple, Michael W. (1996). *Cultural politics and education*. New York: Teachers College Press.

Apple, Michael W., & Beane, James A. (Eds.). (1995). *Democratic schools*. Alexandria, VA: Association for Supervision and Curriculum Development.

Beane, James A. (1975). The case for core in the middle school. *Middle School Journal, 6*(4), 33–34.

Beane, James A. (1976). Options for interdisciplinary teams. *Dissemination Services on the Middle Grades, 7*(3), 1–6.

Beane, James A. (1980). The general education we need. *Educational Leadership, 37*(4), 307–308.

Beane, James A. (1990a). *Affect in the curriculum: Toward democracy, dignity, and diversity*. New York: Teachers College Press.

Beane, James A. (1990b). *A middle school curriculum: From rhetoric to reality*. Columbus, OH: National Middle School Association.

Beane, James A. (1991). The middle school: Natural home of integrated curriculum. *Educational Leadership, 49*(2), 9–13.

Beane, James A. (1992). Turning the floor over: Reflections on *A Middle School Curriculum*. *Middle School Journal, 23*(3), 34–40.

Beane, James A. (1993a). *A middle school curriculum: From rhetoric to reality* (rev. ed.). Columbus, OH: National Middle School Association.

Beane, James A. (1993b). Pentimento, Judi! Pentimento. In Tom Dickinson (Ed.), *Readings in middle school curriculum* (pp. 213–215). Columbus, OH: National Middle School Association.

Beane, James A. (Ed.). (1995a). *Toward a coherent curriculum*, 1995 Yearbook of the Association for Supervision and Curriculum Development. Alexandria, VA: Association for Supervision and Curriculum Development.

Beane, James A. (1995b). Curriculum integration and the disciplines of knowledge. *Phi Delta Kappan, 76,* 616–622.

Beane, James A., & Lipka, Richard P. (1986). *Self-concept, self-esteem, and the curriculum.* New York: Teachers College Press.

Beane, James A., Toepfer, Conrad F., Jr., & Alessi, Samuel J., Jr. (1986). *Curriculum planning and development.* Boston: Allyn & Bacon.

Bellack, Arno A. (1956). Selection and organization of curriculum content. In *What shall the high schools teach?,* 1956 Yearbook of the Association for Supervision and Curriculum Development. Washington, DC: Association for Supervision and Curriculum Development.

Bellack, Arno A., & Kliebard, Herbert M. (1971). Curriculum for integration of disciplines. In Lee C. Deighton (Ed.), *The encyclopedia of education* (pp. 585–590). New York: Macmillan.

Bernstein, Basil. (1975). *Class, codes, and control: Vol. 3. Towards a theory of educational transmissions* (2nd ed.) London: Routledge & Kegan Paul.

Bestor, Arthur E. (1953). *Educational wastelands: The retreat from learning in our public schools.* Urbana: University of Illinois Press.

Bissex, Glenda L., & Bullock, Richard, H. (Eds.). (1987). *Seeing for ourselves.* Portsmouth, NH: Heineman.

Bliss, Henry F. (1929). *The organization of knowledge and the system of the sciences.* New York: Holt.

Bloom, Allan. (1987). *The closing of the American mind.* New York: Simon & Schuster.

Bond, Horace Mann. (1935). The curriculum and the Negro child. *Journal of Negro Education, 4,* 159–168.

Bossing, Nelson L. (1935). *Progressive methods of teaching in high school.* New York: Houghton Mifflin.

Brady, Marion. (1989). *What's worth teaching? Selecting, organizing, and integrating knowledge.* Albany: State University of New York Press.

Brady, Marion. (1995). A supradisciplinary curriculum. In J. A. Beane (Ed.), *Toward a coherent curriculum*, 1995 Yearbook of the Association for Supervision and Curriculum Development (pp. 26–33). Alexandria, VA: Association for Supervision and Curriculum Development.

Brameld, Theodore. (1944). Progressive education on the firing line. *Current History*, pp. 95–100.

Brantlinger, Ellen, Majd-Jabbari, Massoumeh, & Guskin, Samuel L. (1996). Self-interest and liberal educational discourse: How ideology works for middle-class mothers. *American Educational Research Journal, 33,* 571–598.

Brazee, Edward, & Capelluti, Joseph. (1995). *Dissolving boundaries: toward an inte-*

grative middle school curriculum. Columbus, OH: National Middle School Association.

Bredekamp, Susan. (1987). *Developmentally appropriate practice in early childhood programs: Serving children from birth through age 8.* Washington, DC: National Association for the Education of Young Children.

Brodhagen, Barbara L. (1994). Assessing and reporting student progress in an integrative curriculum. *Teaching and Change, 1,* 238–254.

Brodhagen, Barbara L. (1995). The situation made us special. In Michael W. Apple & James A. Beane (Eds.), *Democratic schools* (pp. 83–100). Alexandria, VA: Association for Supervision and Curriculum Development.

Brodhagen, Barbara L., Weilbacher, Gary, & Beane, James A. (1992). Living in the future. *Dissemination Services on the Middle Grades, 23*(9), 1–6.

Brooks, Jacqueline Grennon, & Brooks, Martin G. (1993). *The case for constructivist classrooms.* Alexandria, VA: Association for Supervision and Curriculum Development.

Brophy, Jere, & Alleman, Janet. (1991). A caveat: Curriculum integration isn't always a good idea. *Educational Leadership, 49*(2), p. 66.

Bruner, Jerome S. (1960). *The process of education.* Cambridge, MA: Harvard University Press.

Bruner, Jerome S. (1971). *The Process of Education* reconsidered. In Robert R. Leeper (Ed.), *Dare to care/dare to act: Racism and education* (pp. 19–30). Washington, DC: Association for Supervision and Curriculum Development.

Burton, William H. (1952). *The guidance of learning activities.* New York: Appleton-Century-Crofts.

Cadman, Paul F. (1931). An integrated curriculum for the integration of children from the standpoint of community participation. *National Education Association Proceedings and Addresses* (pp. 476–477). Washington, DC: National Education Association.

Caine, Renata, & Caine, Geoffrey. (1991). *Teaching and the human brain.* Alexandria, VA: Association for Supervision and Curriculum Development.

Capehart, Bertis E. (1958). Illustrative courses and programs in selected secondary schools. In Nelson B. Henry (Ed.), *The integration of educational experiences,* 57th Yearbook of the National Society for the Study of Education, Part II (pp. 195–217). Chicago: University of Chicago Press.

Cary, M. E. (1937). *Integration and the high school curriculum.* Unpublished doctoral dissertation, Ohio State University, Columbus.

Caswell, Hollis L., & Campbell, Doak S. (1935). *Curriculum development.* New York: American Book.

Childs, John L., & Dewey, John. (1933). The social-economic situation and education. In William H. Kilpatrick et al., *The educational frontier* (pp. 32–72). New York: Century.

Citizens for Excellence in Education. (1992). *Reinventing America's schools: A practical guide to components of restructuring and non-traditional education* (Vol. 2). Costa Mesa, CA: Author.

Clarke, John H., & Agne, Russell M. (1996). *Interdisciplinary high school teaching: Strategies for integrated learning.* Boston: Allyn & Bacon.

Connell, R. W. (1993). *Schools and social justice*. Philadelphia, PA: Temple University Press.

Corey, Stephen M., et al. (1942). *General education in the American high school*. New York: Scott, Foresman.

Cross, Beverly E. (1995). The case for culturally coherent curriculum. In James A. Beane (Ed.), *Toward a coherent curriculum*, 1995 Yearbook of the Association for Supervision and Curriculum Development (pp. 71–86). Alexandria, VA: Association for Supervision and Curriculum Development.

Curriculum Commission of the National Council of Teachers of English. (1935). *An experience curriculum in English*. New York: Appleton-Century.

Daniel, Walter G. (1932). The curriculum. *Journal of Negro Education, 1,* 277–303.

Daniel, Walter G. (1940). The aims of secondary education and the adequacy of the curriculum of the negro secondary school. *Journal of Negro Education, 9,* 465–473.

DeBoer, Jon. J. (1936). Integration: A return to first principles. *School and Society, 43,* 246–253.

DeGarmo, Charles. (1895). *Herbart and the Herbartians*. London: Heineman.

Delpit, Lisa. (1995). *Other people's children: Cultural conflict in the classroom*. New York: New Press.

Dewey, John. (1902). *The child and the curriculum*. Chicago: University of Chicago Press.

Dewey, John. (1910). *How we think*. Boston: Heath.

Dewey, John. (1913). *Interest and effort in education*. Boston: Houghton Mifflin.

Dewey, John. (1915). *The school and society* (rev. ed.). Chicago: University of Chicago Press. (Original work published 1900)

Dewey, John. (1916). *Democracy and education*. New York: Macmillan.

Dewey, John. (1938). *Experience and education*. Bloomington, IN: Kappa Delta Pi.

Dix, Lester. (1936). Integration in the Lincoln School philosophy. *Teachers College Record, 37,* 363–371.

Drake, Susan. (1993). *Planning integrated curriculum: The call to adventure*. Alexandria, VA: Association for Supervision and Curriculum Development.

Dressel, Paul L. (1958). The meaning and significance of integration. In Nelson B. Henry (Ed.), *The integration of educational experiences*, 57th Yearbook of the National Society for the Study of Education, Part II (pp. 3–25). Chicago: University of Chicago Press.

Dutton, Samuel T., & Snedden, David. (1912). *The administration of public education*. New York: Macmillan.

Edelsky, Carole, Altmeyer, Bess, & Flores, Barbara. (1991). *Whole language: What's the difference?* Portsmouth, NH: Heineman.

Ehrenreich, Barbara. (1989). *Fear of falling: The inner life of the middle class*. New York: Random House.

Faunce, Roland C., & Bossing, Nelson L. (1951). *Developing the core curriculum*. New York: Prentice-Hall.

Fogarty, Robin. (1991). *The mindful school: How to integrate the curricula*. Glen Elyn, IL: Skylight.

Ford, G. W., & Pugno, Lawrence (Eds.). (1964). *The structure of knowledge and the curriculum.* Chicago: Rand McNally.

Gardner, Howard, & Boix-Mansilla, Veronica. (1994). Teaching for understanding—and beyond. *Teachers College Record, 96,* 198–218.

Gehrke, Nathalie. (1991). Exploration of teacher development of integrative curriculums. *Journal of Curriculum and Supervision, 6,* 107–117.

George, Paul S. (1996). The integrated curriculum: Problems and pitfalls. *Middle School Journal, 28,* 12–19.

Giles, H. H. (1941). *Teacher–pupil planning.* New York: Harper & Brothers.

Giles, H. H., McCutchen, S. F., & Zechiel, A. N. (1942). *Exploring the curriculum.* New York: Harper & Brothers.

Gleeson, Denis, & Whitty, Geoff. (1976). *Developments in social studies teaching.* London: Open Books.

Goodson, Ivor (Ed.). (1985). *Social histories of the secondary school curriculum: Subjects for study.* London and Philadelphia: Falmer.

Graebner, William. (1988). *The engineering of consent: Democracy as social authority in the 20th century.* Madison: University of Wisconsin Press.

Hanna, Lavone A., Potter, Gladys, L., & Hagaman, Neva. (1955). *Unit teaching in the elementary school.* New York: Holt, Rinehart & Winston.

Hanna, Paul R. (1946). Education for the larger community. *Educational Leadership, 4*(2), 27–33.

Hanna, Paul R., & Lang, Arch D. (1950). Integration. In Walter S. Monroe (Ed.), *The encyclopedia of educational research* (pp. 592–600). New York: Macmillan.

Hart, Leslie. (1983). *Human brain and human learning.* New York: Longman.

Harter, Paula D., & Gehrke, Nathalie J. (1989). Integrative curriculum: A kaleidoscope of alternatives. *Educational Horizons, 68*(1), 12–17.

Harvard University, Committee on the Objectives of General Education in a Free Society. (1945). *General education in a free society.* Cambridge, MA: Harvard University Press.

Hatfield, W. Wilbur. (1935). *An experience curriculum in English: A report of the Curriculum Commission of the National Council of Teachers of English.* New York: Appleton-Century.

Henry, George H. (1956). Foundations of general education in the high school. In *What shall the high schools teach?* 1956 Yearbook of the Association for Supervision and Curriculum Development (pp. 127–175). Washington, DC: Association for Supervision and Curriculum Development.

Henry, Nelson B. (Ed.). (1958). *The integration of educational experiences,* 57th Yearbook of the National Society for the Study of Education. Chicago: University of Chicago Press.

Hiebert, Elfrieda H., & Fisher, Charles W. (1990). Whole language: Three themes for the future. *Educational Leadership, 47*(6), 62–63.

Hirsch, E. D., Jr. (1987). *Cultural literacy.* Boston: Houghton Mifflin.

Hirst, P. H., & Peters, R. S. (1970). *The logic of education.* London: Routledge & Kegan Paul.

Hirst, Paul. (1974). *Knowledge and the curriculum.* London: Routledge & Kegan Paul.

Hock, Louise, & Hill, Thomas. (1960). *The general education class in the secondary school*. New York: Holt-Rinehart.

Hopkins, L. Thomas. (1929). *Curriculum principles and practices*. New York: Sanborn.

Hopkins, L. Thomas. (1932). Editor's introduction. In Francis Sweeney, Emily F. Barry, & Alice E. Schoelkopf, *Western youth meets Eastern culture: A study of the integration of social studies, English, and art in the junior high school* (pp. vii–viii). New York: Teachers College Press.

Hopkins, L. Thomas. (1935). Arguments favoring integration. *Teachers College, 36,* 604–612.

Hopkins, L. Thomas. (1941). *Interaction: The democratic process*. New York: Heath.

Hopkins, L. Thomas. (1954). *The emerging self in school and home*. New York: Harper & Brothers.

Hopkins, L. Thomas. (1955). *The core program: Integration and interaction*. New York: Board of Education of the City of New York.

Hopkins, L. Thomas, & Armentrout, W. D. (1931). Principles of integration. In *Five unifying factors in American education*, Ninth Yearbook of the Department of Superintendence of the National Education Association (pp. 367–378). Washington, DC: National Education Association.

Hopkins, L. Thomas, and others. (1937). *Integration: Its meaning and application*. New York: Appleton-Century.

Hullfish, H. Gordon. (1933). The school: Its task and its administration. In William H. Kilpatrick et al., *The educational frontier* (pp. 160–192). New York: Century.

Informal Committee of the Progressive Education Association on Evaluation of Newer Practices in Education. (1941). *New methods vs. old in American education*. New York: Bureau of Publications, Teachers College, Columbia University.

Inglis, Alexander. (1918). *Principles of secondary education*. New York: Houghton Mifflin.

Ingram, James B. (1979). *Curriculum integration and lifelong education*. Oxford, UK: UNESCO Institute for Education and Pergamon.

Iran-Nejad, Asghar, McKeachie, Wilbert J., & Berliner, David C. (1990). The multisource nature of learning: An introduction, *Review of Educational Research, 60,* 509–515.

Jacobs, Heidi Hayes (Ed.). (1989). *Interdisciplinary curriculum: Design and implementation*. Alexandria, VA: Association for Supervision and Curriculum Development.

Jacobs, Heidi Hayes, & Borland, James. (1986). The interdisciplinary concept model. *Gifted Child Quarterly, 30,* 159–163.

James, Charity. (1972). *Young lives at stake*. New York: Agathon.

Jenkins, F. C. (1947). *The southern study: Cooperative study for the improvement of education*. Durham, NC: Duke University Press.

Jenkins, John M., & Tanner, Daniel. (1992). *Restructuring for an interdisciplinary curriculum*. Reston, VA: National Association of Secondary School Principals.

Kilpatrick, William H. (1918). The project method. *Teachers College Record, 19,* 319–335.

Kilpatrick, William H. (1926). *Education for a changing civilization*. New York: Macmillan.

Kilpatrick, William H. and others.(1933). *The educational frontier.* New York: Century.
Kilpatrick, William H. (1934). The essentials of the activity movement. *Progressive Education, 11,* 346–359.
Kilpatrick, William H. (1936). *Remaking the curriculum.* New York: Newsome.
King, Arthur R., & Brownell, John A. (1966). *The curriculum and the disciplines of knowledge: A theory of curriculum practice.* New York: Wiley.
Klein, Julie Thompson. (1990). *Interdisciplinarity: History, theory, and practice.* Detroit: Wayne State University Press.
Klein, Julie Thompson, & Doty, William G. (1994). *Interdisciplinary studies today.* San Francisco: Jossey-Bass.
Kliebard, Herbert M. (1984). The decline of humanistic studies in the American school curriculum. In Benjamin Ladner (Ed.), *The humanities in precollegiate education,* 83rd Yearbook of the National Society for the Study of Education (pp. 7–30). Chicago: University of Chicago Press.
Kliebard, Herbert M. (1986). *The struggle for the American curriculum: 1893–1958.* Boston: Routledge & Kegan Paul.
Kovalik, Susan. (1994). *ITI: The model, integrated thematic instruction* (3rd ed.). Susan Kovalik and Associates.
Krogh, Suzanne. (1990). *The integrated early childhood curriculum.* New York: McGraw-Hill.
Krug, Edward A. (1957). *Curriculum planning* (rev. ed.). New York: Harper & Brothers.
Kuhn, Thomas S. (1962). *The structure of scientific revolutions.* Chicago: University of Chicago Press.
Lounsbury, John H., & Vars, Gordon F. (1978). *A curriculum for the middle school years.* New York: Harper & Row.
Lurry, Lucille L., & Alberty, Elsie J. (1957). *Developing the high school core program.* New York: Macmillan.
Macdonald, James B. (1971). Curriculum integration. In Lee C. Deighton (Ed.), *The encyclopedia of education* (pp. 590–593). New York: Macmillan.
Macdonald, James B., Andersen, Dan W., & May, Frank B. (1965). *Strategies of curriculum development: Selected writings of the late Virgil E. Herrick.* Columbus, OH: Merrill.
Martin-Kniep, Giselle O., Feige, Diane M., & Soodak, Leslie C. (1995). Curriculum integration: An expanded view of an abused idea. *Journal of Curriculum and Supervision, 10,* 227–249.
Martinello, Marian L., & Cook, Gillian E. (1994). *Interdisciplinary inquiry in teaching and learning.* New York: Macmillan.
Marzano, Robert J., Pickering, Diane, & Brandt, Ron. (1990). Integrating instruction programs through dimensions of learning. *Educational Leadership, 47*(5), 17–24.
McMurry, Charles A. (Ed.). (1895). *First yearbook of the Herbart Society.* Bloomington, IL: Public School Publishing.
McMurry, Frank M. (1927). Some recollections of the past forty years of education. *Peabody Journal of Education, 4,* 325–332.
Meeth, Richard L. (1978). Interdisciplinary studies: A matter of definition. *Change, 10,* 10.

Meriam, Junius L. (1920). *Child life and the curriculum*. Yonkers-on-Hudson, NY: World Book.

Mickelson, John M. (1957). What does research say about the effectiveness of the core curriculum? *School Review, 65*, 144–160.

Miller, John P., Cassie, J. R., & Drake, Susan. (1990). *Holistic learning: A teacher's guide to integrated studies*. Toronto: Ontario Institute for Studies in Education.

Monroe, Paul. (1912). *Cyclopedia of education*. New York: Macmillan.

Mursell, James. (1955). *Principles of democratic education*. New York: Norton.

Nagel, Nancy G. (1996). *Learning through real-world problem solving*. Thousand Oaks, CA: Corwin.

National Association of Secondary School Principals. (1996). *Breaking ranks: Changing an American institution*. Reston, VA: Author.

National Education Association. (1893). *Report of the Committee on Secondary School Studies*. Washington, DC: U.S. Government Printing Office.

National Education Association. (1895). *Report of the Committee of Fifteen on Elementary Education, with the reports of the sub-committees: On the training of teachers; on the correlation of studies in elementary education; on the organization of city school systems*. New York: American Book.

National Education Association. (1918). *Cardinal principles of secondary education: A report of the Commission on the Reorganization of Secondary Education*. Washington, DC: U.S. Government Printing Office.

Newman, Judith M. (1990). *Finding our own way*. Portsmouth, NH: Heineman.

Newman, Katherine S. (1988). *Fear of falling: The experience of downward mobility in the American middle class*. New York: Random House.

Noar, Gertrude. (1966). *The teacher and integration*. Washington, DC: National Education Association.

Oberholtzer, E. E. (1934). Comments by leaders in the field. In G. M. Whipple (Ed.), *The activity movement*, 33rd Yearbook of the National Society for the Study of Education, Part II (pp. 136–142). Bloomington, IL: Public School Publishing.

Oberholtzer, E. (1937). *An integrated curriculum in practice*. New York: Teachers College Press.

Orner, Mimi. (1992). Interrupting the calls for student voice in "liberatory" education: A feminist poststructural perspective. In Carmen Luke & Jennifer Gore (Eds.), *Feminisms and critical pedagogy* (pp. 74–89). New York: Routledge.

Pace, Glenellen (Ed.). (1995). *Whole learning in the middle school*. Norwood, MA: Christopher-Gordon.

Pate, Elizabeth, Homestead, Elaine, & McGinnis, Karen. (1996). *Making integrated curriculum work: Teachers, students, and the quest for a a coherent curriculum*. New York: Teachers College Press.

Pearson, P. David. (1989). Reading the whole language movement. *The Elementary School Journal, 90*, 230–241.

Popkewitz, Thomas S. (Ed.). (1987). *The formation of school subjects: The struggle for creating an American institution*. New York: Falmer.

Powell, Richard, Skoog, Gerald, Troutman, Porter, & Jones, Graig. (1996, April). *Standing on the edge of middle level curriculum reform: Factors influencing the sustainability of a non-linear integrative learning environment.* Paper presented at the Annual Meeting of the American Educational Research Association, New York.

Ravitch, Diane. (1995). *National standards in American education: A citizen's guide.* Washington, DC: Brookings Institution.

Ravitch, Diane, & Finn, Chester E., Jr. (1987). *What do our 17-year-olds know?* New York: Harper & Row.

Rickover, Hyman G. (1959). *Education and freedom.* New York: Dutton.

Roth, Kathleen. (1994). Second thoughts about interdisciplinary studies. *American Educator, 18,* 44–48.

Routman, Regie. (1991). *Invitations: Changing as teachers and learners K–12.* Portsmouth, NH: Heineman.

Rugg, Harold. (1936). *American life and the school curriculum.* Boston: Ginn.

Rugg, Harold (Ed.). (1939). *Democracy and the curriculum,* 3rd Yearbook of the John Dewey Society. New York: Appleton-Century.

Rugg, Harold, & Shumaker, Anne. (1928). *The child-centered school.* New York: World Book.

SCANS, The Secretary's Commission on Achieving Necessary Skills. (1992). *Learning a living: A blueprint for high performance.* Washington, DC: U.S. Department of Labor.

Schubert, William H. (1986). *Curriculum: Perspective, paradigm, and possibility.* New York: Macmillan.

Shoemaker, Betty Jean Eklund. (1991). Education 2000: Integrated curriculum. *Phi Delta Kappan, 72,* 793–796.

Siskin, Leslie Santee, & Little, Judith Warren. (1995). *The subjects in question: Departmental organization and the high school.* New York: Teachers College Press.

Siu-Runyan, Yvonne, & Faircloth, V. (Eds.). (1995). *Beyond separate subjects: Middle school curriculum for the 21st century.* Norwood, MA: Christopher-Gordon.

Smith, B. Othanel, Stanley, William O., & Shores, J. H. (1950). *Fundamentals of curriculum development.* New York: Harcourt, Brace, & World.

Smith, Meredith. (1921). An educational experiment: The community project. *Survey, 46,* 301–304.

Smith, Meredith. (1927). *Education and the integration of behavior* (Contributions to Education, No. 261). New York, Teachers College, Columbia University.

Smith, Mortimer B. (1949). *And madly teach: A layman looks at public school education.* Chicago: Henry Regnery.

Smith, William A. (1935). Integration: Potentially the most significant forward step in the history of secondary education. *California Journal of Secondary Education, 10,* 269–272.

Spencer, Herbert. (1870). *First principles of a new system of philosophy* (2nd ed.). New York: Appleton.

Stevenson, Chris, & Carr, Judy F. (Eds.). (1993). *Integrative studies in the middle grades: Dancing through walls.* New York: Teachers College Press.

Stratemeyer, Florence, Forkner, Hamden L., McKim, Margaret G., & Passow, A. Harry. (1947). *Developing a curriculum for modern living.* New York: Teachers College, Columbia University.

Sweeney, Francis E. (1936). Integration in the junior high school. *Teachers College Record, 37,* 399–405.

Sweeney, Francis E., Barry, Emily F., & Schoelkopf, Alice E. (1932). *Western youth meets eastern culture: A study in the integration of social studies, English, and art in the junior high school.* New York: Teachers College Press.

Sylwester, Robert. (1995). *A celebration of neurons.* Alexandria, VA: Association for Supervision and Curriculum Development.

Tanner, Daniel. (1989). A brief historical perspective of the struggle for an integrative curriculum. *Educational Horizons, 68,* 6–11.

Tanner, Daniel, & Tanner, Laurel N. (1980). *Curriculum development: Theory into practice.* New York: Macmillan.

Van Til, William. (1946). Exploring educational frontiers. In *Leadership through supervision,* 1946 Yearbook of the Association for Supervision and Curriculum Development. Washington, DC: Association for Supervision and Curriculum Development.

Vars, Gordon F. (Ed.). (1969). *Common learnings: Core and interdisciplinary team approaches.* Scranton, PA: Intext.

Vars, Gordon F. (1987). *Interdisciplinary teaching: Why and how.* Columbus, OH: National Middle School Association.

Vars, Gordon F. (1991). Integrated curriculum in historical perspective. *Educational Leadership, 49*(1), 14–15.

Vars, Gordon F. (1993). *Interdisciplinary teaching: Why & how* (2nd ed.). Columbus, OH: National Middle School Association.

Vars, Gordon F. (1996). The effects of interdisciplinary curriculum and instruction. In Peters S. Hlebowitsh & William G. Wraga (Eds.), *Annual review of research for school leaders, part II: transcending traditional subject matter lines: Interdisciplinary curriculum and instruction* (pp. 147–164). Reston, VA: National Association of Secondary School Principals, and New York: Scholastic.

Ward, James M., Suttle, John E., & Otto, Henry J. (1960). *The curriculum integration concept applied in the elementary school.* Austin, TX: University of Texas Press.

Waskin, Yvonne, & Parrish, Louise. (1957). *Teacher pupil planning for better classroom learning.* New York: Pitman.

Watson, Goodwin. (1931). An integrated curriculum for the integration of children from the standpoint of psychology. In *National Education Association Proceedings and Addresses* (pp. 472–476). Washington, DC: National Education Association.

Wells, Cyrene. (1995). *Literacies lost: When students move from a progressive middle school to a traditional high school.* New York: Teachers College Press.

Wesley, Charles H. (1941). Education for citizenship in a democracy. *Journal of Negro Education, 10,* 68–78.

Williams, Raymond. (1961). *The long revolution.* London: Chatto & Windus.

Wisconsin Public Telecommunications for Education. (1992). *Exploring curriculum options, part II* (video). Madison, WI: Author.

Wood, George H. (1992). *Schools that work.* New York: Dutton.

Wraga, William G. (1991). The core curriculum in the middle school. *Middle School Journal, 23*(2), 16–23.

Wraga, William G. (1993). The interdisciplinary imperative for citizenship education. *Theory and Research in Social Education, 21*, 201–231.

Wright, Grace S. (1950). *Core curriculum in public high schools: An inquiry into practices, 1949* (Bulletin 1950, No. 5, Office of Education). Washington, DC: U.S. Government Printing Office.

Wright, Grace S. (1958). *Block-time classes and the core program in the junior high school* (Bulletin 1958, No. 6, Office of Education). Washington, DC: U.S. Government Printing Office.

Wrightstone, J. Wayne. (1935). Evaluation of the integrated curriculum in the upper grades. *Elementary School Journal, 35*, 583–587.

Wrightstone, J. Wayne. (1936). *Appraisal of experimental high school practices.* New York: Bureau of Publications, Teachers College, Columbia University.

Wrightstone, J. Wayne. (1938). *Appraisal of newer elementary school practices.* New York: Bureau of Publications, Teachers College, Columbia University.

Yager, Robert E. (1988). A new focus for school science: STS. *School Science and Mathematics, 88*, 181–190.

Young, Dan, & Gehrke, Nathalie. (1993). Curriculum integration for transcendence: A critical review of recent books on curriculum integration. *Curriculum Inquiry, 23*, 445–454.

Young, Jean Helen. (1991/1992). Curriculum integration: Perceptions of preservice teachers. *Action in Teacher Education, 13*(4), 1–9.

Young, Michael F. D. (1971). An approach to the study of curricula as socially organized knowledge. In Michael F. D. Young (Ed.), *Knowledge and control* (pp. 19–46). London: Collier-Macmillan.

Zapf, Rosalind M. (1959). *Democratic processes in the classroom.* Englewood Cliffs, NJ: Prentice-Hall.

Zemelman, Steven, Daniels, Harvey, & Hyde, Arthur. (1993). *Best practice: New standards for teaching and learning in America's schools.* Portsmouth, NH: Heineman.

Index

About the Author

James A. Beane is a professor in the Department of Interdisciplinary Studies in Curriculum, National College of Education, National–Louis University. He has taught in junior high, middle, and high schools and has been a project director for New York State Regional Education Planning Centers.

Professor Beane is author of *Affect in the Curriculum: Toward Democracy, Dignity and Diversity* and *A Middle School Curriculum: From Rhetoric to Reality*; co-author of *Self-Concept, Self-Esteem and the Curriculum, Curriculum Planning and Development, The Middle School and Beyond,* and *When the Kids Come First: Enhancing Self-Esteem at the Middle Level*; co-editor of *Democratic Schools*; and editor of the 1995 ASCD (Association for Supervision and Curriculum Development) Yearbook, *Toward a Coherent Curriculum.*